CW00642834

Group Dynamics

Basics and Pragmatics
for Practitioners

Norris M. Haynes

Foreword by Joy E. Fopiano

UNIVERSITY PRESS OF AMERICA, ® INC.
Lanham • Boulder • New York • Toronto • Plymouth, UK

Copyright © 2012 by
University Press of America,® Inc.
4501 Forbes Boulevard
Suite 200
Lanham, Maryland 20706
UPA Acquisitions Department (301) 459-3366

Estover Road
Plymouth PL6 7PY
United Kingdom

Library of Congress Control Number: 2011936044
ISBN: 978-0-7618-5697-9 (paperback : alk. paper)
eISBN: 978-0-7618-5698-6

Contents

List of Activities

Foreword

Most of us daily, from the very young to our population of retired and elder persons, participate in a wide variety of group experiences. We gather in groups for play, for work, for fellowship, to learn, and to glean support. We form groups when we are very happy and we form groups as we grieve our pain. We may be organized in groups to provide information, to build community, or to contribute hope. We are social creatures who use language and the sharing of ourselves to move forward with our interests and with our goals. With that, an understanding of how groups work; how they operate; how they can empower may be essential to the graduate student experience. As a graduate school trainer of counselors and psychologists, I believe that a study and understanding of groups and their membership is critical.

Dr. Haynes has prepared a valuable guide for counselors and school psychologists to begin to expand their foundational understanding of groups. It is clear that this narrative could be used as a vital companion to a group course presented as a graduate school learning experience. The book takes the reader beyond an abstract and more theoretical understanding of group dynamics and the specific stages of groups to highly detailed examples of how graduate students' learning develops through this teaching model. Journal reflections prepared by graduate students who were class participants illustrate the power of their individual learning through the conceptual model Dr. Haynes portrays. The reader sees how impactful the exercises and the experience of being a group member concurrently to taking a group dynamics course in this format has been to student participants. Indeed, the accounts presented I found to be stirring.

Graduate students express their surprise at how rapidly the group process moved forward as they join class. Students are able to tie the conceptual model of group development to what they are actually experiencing as a group member. Touched by the disclosures of peer colleagues, relationships have been formed and continued as a result of these specific group experiences. As reader, one can see the sustaining impact these concepts have on students and how useful groups can be when successfully organized and operated in schools and in community.

For over fifteen years Dr. Haynes has been excited to teach classes in group dynamics to graduate students in school counseling, clinical mental health and school psychology. Public school districts and community agencies run groups for children frequently and perhaps not always with clarity of purpose and proper evaluation. In this text, Dr. Haynes supports the new practitioner in learning how to appropriately establish a new group, determine a structure for selecting members, establish how to set goals, and how to gather data to evaluate progress. Groups are designed with purpose, and evaluation is a critical and fundamental component of assessing progress. Further, with great respect to both reader and participant, Dr. Haynes shares how significant sensitive group leadership is to facilitate discovery and growth for individual group members.

Graduate students may recognize some of the activities presented here to illustrate learning goals. However, what becomes clear is how the structure of these experiences weaves to shape a curriculum designed to enhance the training necessary for future counselors and psychologists to become themselves skilled group facilitators. As a trainer of school psychologists, I am pleased to see clear emphasis on data gathering. This, with group analysis, and the evaluation component will allow the field professional to use groups to enhance their understanding of problems and how to create solutions.

We advocate best practice for our field professionals. Superior group experiences may be one vehicle to encourage children who participate to feel safe to express themselves and stretch to reach new goals. Children and youth, now perhaps more than ever, may benefit from joining together to learn that they are not alone in their experience. In these times of worldwide stress, supporting children to be valued contributing members of a group may have especially far reaching impact for their academic learning and personal emotional development.

Professor Haynes has written this book as a practical guide to the understanding, teaching and facilitating of group dynamics in various settings. He does not purport to provide profound analyses or delve deeply into group theory although he does provide an overview of selected theories. The essence and value in this work lie in the understandable and engaging manner in which group dynamics concepts come alive and the multiple audiences to which this work would appeal.

Dr. Joy E. Fopiano

Chapter One

Defining Groups, Types of Groups and Value of Groups

Each individual is in some way influenced by at least one group and most likely by multiple groups simultaneously. For example, a person may be influenced by family members and by close friends at the same time. However, individuals seldom reflect on the multiple and significant influences of groups on their lives. Some groups have lasting impact on individuals, help to shape their personalities and help to chart the course of their lives. Yet groups are not often given the attention nor assigned the importance in the personal lives of individuals that they deserve. In this introductory chapter, an effort is made to establish an understanding of what constitutes a group, explain the composition and purpose of different types of groups, and discuss the value that groups have in the lives of individuals.

DEFINING GROUPS

A group may be defined as, "an entity comprised of individuals who come together for a common purpose and whose behaviors in the group are guided by a set of shared values and norms," (Haynes, 1998). The elements of this definition that separate a group from a crowd or just an assembly of people are: *a common purpose shared values* and *shared norms.*

Common purpose means that the members of the group are participating in the group activities to achieve similar goals. They are motivated to participate in the group process and dynamics by a shared set of desired outcomes.

Shared values means that the members of the group share certain core beliefs about what the structure and essence of the group is and strive to maintain the group's integrity.

1

Shared norms means that the members of the group agree on certain over-arching principles that direct or influence the manner in which the group members behave and interact with one another in the context of the group. In children's groups these are referred to as rules.

A group is different from the collective personalities of the individuals who form the group. It is a unique, dynamic whole that grows out of the interactions among group members in context. The group that is formed has its own identity that is different from the collection of individual identities of the group members. It is acknowledged however, that each individual brings an identity that includes his or her personal history, values, needs and desires to the group. During the group process the individual identity contributes to the dynamics of the group and is influenced by the group process. Sometimes the individual adheres so strongly to his/her identity while in the group that he or she remains an outsider to the group.

TYPES OF GROUPS

There are many different types of groups. For the purpose of discussion, groups have been classified into two broad categories: *functional groups and identity groups.*

Functional Groups are groups that are classified on the basis of what they are designed to do and accomplish. They are defined by their purpose.

1. *T-Groups:* The "T" is for training. T-Groups are sensitivity groups that are designed to increase participants' self-awareness, promote self-growth, enhance sensitivity to the feelings of others and improve one's effectiveness as a group participant. The concepts of training and sensitivity are combined in the notion of "T" groups because the training centers on helping individuals increase their sensitivity to the emotional needs of others in their interpersonal interactions and to their own emotional needs. One may say that these groups are designed to enhance intra-personal intelligence (self-awareness and self-regulation) and interpersonal intelligence (awareness of and interactions with others). A specific type of sensitivity group is the *Encounter Group* that uses verbal or physical confrontation or encounters to promote personal growth.

2. *Counseling Groups:* These groups are designed to help members address specific physical, social, psychological, emotional or behavioral issues. Through the group process, including active listening and feedback, group members are able to confront and address the issues of concern. The desired outcome is usually to change the existing situation to one that is more adaptive and healthy for each member of the group. Examples of counsel-

ing groups are an anger management group and a group for children of divorced parents.

3. *Therapy Groups:* These groups are similar to counseling groups except that the issues tend to be more serious and require a much more experienced and knowledgeable group facilitator. Examples of therapy groups are a group for individuals with eating disorders and a group for individuals with anxiety disorders.

4. *Work Groups:* These groups are designed to accomplish specific tasks on fixed timelines and deliver a clearly expected product at the end of the specified time frame. The group is evaluated on the basis of the quality of the product. Most teams would be classified as work groups. Specific examples of team that are work groups are: a grant writing team where the product would be a grant proposal, a planning and placement team (PPT) in a school where the product would be a an individual education plan (IEP) for a student, or a sports team where the product would be the record at the end of the season.

5. *Focus Groups:* These groups are designed to generate data on the basis of which informed decisions are made. Usually a small group of individuals is convened to discuss a particular topic and to address focused questions on that topic. The responses to the questions, as well as the passion and emotional reactions to the questions and the interactions among group members, are all considered to be important data for decision makers. Examples of focus groups are the group that is convened by a politician to gauge constituents' reactions to a proposed piece of legislation and the group that is assembled by the marketing department of a company to assess consumers' reactions to a product or advertising campaign.

6. *Support Groups:* These are groups that are designed as opportunities for individuals facing similar physical, social, psychological or emotional issues to come together to offer and receive support from one another. Sharing experiences and offering support, serves to inspire hope as members realize that they are not alone and others have faced or are facing similar issues. Members are able learn from the experiences of one another. These groups differ from counseling and therapy groups in that there is no targeted physical, social, psychological or emotional change expected for any member of the group, although a by-product of the support one receives might be such a change. Support groups tend to be more member-directed and led than counseling and therapy groups. Examples of support groups related to alcohol addiction are: Alcoholics Anonymous (AA), Al-Anon and Al-A-teen. Other support groups in school settings may include groups for children of divorced parents and groups for students who have lost a close friend or family member.

7. *Psycho-educational groups:* These are groups that are designed to address students' school-related behaviors and their academic achievement. These

groups are focused specifically on identified issues that may be affecting students' achievement motivation leading to underachievement and school failure. A psycho-educational group process called the Interest, Achievement and Motivation, "I AM" group process is described in chapter ten and an overview of the evaluation of this psycho-educational group process is provided.

Identity Groups are groups that are classified by the nature of the affiliation that members of the groups share with one another.

1. *Membership Groups:* These are groups that involve some form of officially recognized status as a member. Usually these groups require that the participant be inducted or receive official acknowledgement as a member and may, but not necessarily, require a membership fee or membership dues. Additionally, there is often an official membership roster that is revised and updated after a specified period of time. Renewal of membership after a specified period of time is usually also required. Examples of membership groups are: sororities, fraternities and athletic teams.
2. *Reference Groups:* These are groups that do not require official recognition or induction as a member, rather they are groups with whose values, purpose and goals individuals identify. A reference group for some individuals may be a membership group for others. A good example of this would be football or basket ball fans, who are not officially members of sports teams but identify with the sports teams. Therefore, the sports teams may be considered reference groups. Other examples of reference groups include different advocacy groups such as Mothers Against Drunk Driving (MADD) and Green Peace with whose mission and goals many people who are not card-carrying members identify.
3. *Open Groups:* These are groups whose memberships are fluid, and where people are free to join or leave as they choose. There are usually no specific attendance requirements. Support groups are usually open groups.
4. *Closed Groups:* These are groups whose memberships are fixed, and where people are not free to join or leave as they choose. There are usually clear and strict attendance requirements. Counseling and therapy groups are usually closed groups.
5. *In-Groups:* These are groups that are considered to include the most popular individuals. It is considered desirable to belong to these groups. Among school-aged children, in-groups tend to wield a great deal of influence and power. They often exclude individuals whom the members of the in-group consider to lack certain traits that they feel important for membership. These groups are said to be the popular groups or the groups with the popular people.

6. *Out-Groups:* These groups include individuals who are excluded or denied membership by members of the in-group. Members of this group are considered to be less popular and are deemed to occupy a lower status in the social hierarchy. Sometimes members of this group suffer ridicule, rejection, ostracism and even bullying by members of the in-group. This is a particularly challenging issue among school-age children.

7. *Family Groups:* These are groups that include individuals who are related by blood, adoption or election. These groups are usually divided into nuclear, primary, and extended family groups. Nuclear family groups usually include parents and children. Primary family groups typically include family members who share the same household or, if they do not share the same household, are deemed to play a significant role in the daily lives of family members. Extended family groups usually include family members who are not nuclear or primary family members.

8. *Friendship Groups:* These are groups that include individuals who are friends and who may share time, activities, interests and actual or virtual space regularly or periodically. Social networking websites such as MySpace, Face book, Blogosphere and Twitter have considerably expanded the reach of friendship groups. In fact, it may be that these internet connections may deserve a separate group classification, such as Internet Networking Groups, but for now they are being included as friendship groups.

VALUE OF GROUPS FOR INDIVIDUALS

Some of the positive experiences that individuals have through their participation in groups are that individuals:

- Receive support, encouragement and validation during self-exploration and growth;
- Learn by observing the behaviors and consequences of the actions of others;
- Achieve a sense of belonging and connectedness;
- Share common problems; and
- Receive feedback that can help in personal growth and development.

The benefits that individuals receive from groups are supported through the following group factors or processes:

Support for Catharsis: Groups provide an opportunity for an individual to "emote" or express his or her deep and true feelings about issues, among group members who listen and empathize. As a result, the individual

experiences release, relief and freedom from emotional and psychological pain, enabling the individual to experience personal grow.

Sharing of Information: Group members share information which expands the
perspective, knowledge, awareness and interests of individuals in the group.

Providing Hope: As group members share their stories and provide feedback
and support to one another, they come to demonstrate resilience, determi-
nation, strength and optimism. Individuals who may otherwise despair may
become hopeful and more determined than ever to succeed.

Giving of Feedback: Feedback allows group members to become more aware of
their interpersonal interactions, and to see themselves as others in the group
may see them. This may lead to helpful changes in attitudes and behaviors.

Promoting Bonding: Group members may experience a feeling of connectedness, togetherness and cohesion. This allows individuals in the group to derive a sense of affiliation and identification with members of the group, perhaps filling a personal need by reducing feelings of isolation and aloneness.

Promoting Interpersonal Skills: Groups help individual members develop or
refine their social interaction skills by learning how to read and respond
appropriately to social cues.

Promoting Intrapersonal Skills: Groups help individuals develop or refine
their self-awareness and self-regulation skills by identifying internal emotional cues and learning how to regulate, manage and express their emotions appropriately.

Allowing Re-enactment: Some groups provide the opportunity for group
members to re-enact family dynamics, as well other relationships outside
of the family. This enables individuals to achieve catharsis and therapeutic
release.

Disclosing of Universality: Groups help members realize that they are not
alone in experiencing certain issues and that others share these issues as
well. Thus, members can learn coping strategies and problem solving approaches from others who are in the same or similar predicament.

Activity # 1: The Many Circles of

"The Many Circles of" activity uses a web that has seven circles. In the center is
an inner circle that represents the individual's most significant or most important
group affiliation. Connected by straight lines to the inner center circle are six
outer circles that represent other groups with which the individual is affiliated.

In this activity, the participant writes his or her full name, including middle
initial if he or she has one, on the line following the words "The Many Circles
of." The individual is then required to identify the group that he or she considers the most important group to which he or she belongs. The name of that
group is written in the inner center circle. Next, in each of the six outer circles
the individual writes the name of another significant group to which he or
she belongs, completing all six circles if possible. The individual is invited to

rank each of the groups in the outer circles, reflecting the group's influence or importance to the individual.

Then, in small discussion groups, each individual shares his or her circles starting with the larger inner circle sharing the following information about each group:

- Group values and norms
- The nature of interpersonal interactions among group members
- What the individual likes most and likes least about the group
- The influence of the group on the individual

After sharing these four points, the members of the discussion group ask open-ended and close-ended questions (for information on open-ended and close-ended questions, see chapter five on group process) and provide feedback to the individual who has just shared information about the groups in his/her circles.

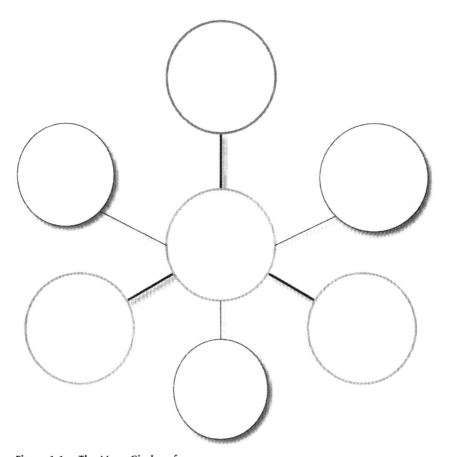

Figure 1.1.   The Many Circles of_____.

Chapter Two

Stages of Group Development

Individuals go through several stages of development during the course of their lives. These stages include: infancy, early childhood, late childhood, early adolescence, late adolescence, early adulthood, middle adulthood, late adulthood and death. With each stage, the individual experiences physical, social, psychological, emotional and cognitive changes. Individuals progress through these stages at different rates and adapt and adjust to the changes at each stage differently than others.

Groups, like individuals, go through stages of development experiencing changes in leadership, interpersonal interactions, roles, communication structures, and power structures. As groups progress through their stages, group members undergo commensurate social, psychological, emotional and cognitive changes. The values of groups become more salient to the individual and the factors of groups that promote change begin to make a difference.

Most groups go through four or five stages of development depending on whose perspective of group development one may choose to use. Table 2.1 provides a summary of five major perspectives on the stages of group development. Though the names of the stages differ, a close examination of each theoretical framework reveals the theorists essentially agree on the basic elements of stages. Below is a realignment of the theoretical perspectives presented in table 2.1 with the essential characteristics of each stage.

Table 2.1. Perspectives on Stages of Group Development.

Theorists	Stage One	Stage Two	Stage Three	Stage Four	Stage Five
Corey & Corey (1997)	Initial	Transition	Working	Ending	
Tuckman and Jensen (1965)	Forming	Storming	Norming	Performing	Adjourning
Wheelan (1994)	Dependency and Inclusion	Counter Dependency and Fight	Trust	Working	Termination
Kottler (2001)	Induction	Experimental Engagement	Cohesive Engagement	Disengagement	
Yalom (1995)	Orientation and Search for Meaning	Conflict, Dominance and Rebellion	Cohesiveness		

STAGE ONE: INITIAL, FORMING, DEPENDENCY AND INCLUSION INDUCTION, ORIENTATION AND SEARCH FOR MEANING

During stage one interpersonal interactions are tentative, superficial, lacking confidence and uncertain. There is an absence of trust among members. Consequently, they look to the assigned leader for direction and guidance. Members are compliant and participation tends to be limited to a few members who are more vocal than others. Leadership is centered on the assigned leader. Group members are concerned with being included in the group and not saying or doing anything that may "rock the boat" and result in rejection. Conformity tends to be high and conflict low or non-existent. Member roles are unclear and undefined. Communication structure tends to be centralized with information among members being filtered through the assigned leader. Members typically communicate in a tentative and relatively polite manner. Power (defined as the ability to influence the behavior of others) tends to be concentrated in the assigned leader.

STAGE TWO: TRANSITION, STORMING, COUNTER DEPENDENCY AND FIGHT, EXPERIMENTAL ENGAGEMENT, CONFLICT DOMINANCE AND REBELLION

During stage two interpersonal interactions are more substantive, confident and assertive. As conformity declines, conflicts arise due to disagreements and different points of view. Conflict takes different forms and does not necessarily find expression in stridency, name calling and vociferous debate. It may take the form of mild confrontation and disagreements. There is wider participation in the group process. The assigned leader is challenged and new leadership begins to emerge. Subgroups and cliques begin to form. Member roles begin to emerge and become clear. The communication structure begins to become less centralized and more distributed as does the power within the group. Through the conflicts and the efforts to resolve these conflicts the group moves to a new level of engagement that advances the group process to stage three.

STAGE THREE: NORMING, TRUST, COHESIVE ENGAGEMENT, COHESIVENESS

During stage three, interpersonal interactions are based on trust and openness. Members feel that they can be open, free and confident in expressing their thoughts, ideas and feelings. The formation of subgroups may continue or become more solidified as the group becomes more tolerant and accepting of differences and coalitions within the larger group. There is more focused awareness of and attention to others, not just on verbal expressions but also on non-verbal behaviors. Group confidence increases as members begin to trust that members are being candid about what they feel and believe. There is a sense that group members are more genuine and believable. Group cohesion increases, meaning that group members feel more connected, they bond more and there is more buy-in to the purpose and goals of the group. It does not mean that no more disagreements or conflicts arise. However, when conflicts and disagreements arise at this stage, there are more constructive and helpful approaches to addressing them recognizing that "we are in this together." The assigned leader's role continues to become less directive and less prominent and new leadership continues to emerge among group members. The communication structure continues to become even more decentralized with members communicating directly with one another, making more eye contact and addressing one another more in the second person "you" as opposed to in the third person "he" or "she."

STAGE FOUR: PERFORMING, WORKING

During stage four, the work of the group gets done. A group's work depends on the type of group it is and the purpose and goals of the group. It is in stage four that the group focuses more intently on accomplishing its goals. Interpersonal interactions are deep, open, and very substantive. Members no longer hold back in sharing their thoughts and feelings. Feedback is characterized by genuine caring and concern for each member's well-being and members receive feedback without defensiveness and resentment. In sensitivity groups, counseling groups and therapy groups, intrapersonal focus is also heightened. Members deepen their self-reflections, consider the feedback they receive and incorporate feedback elements they deem to be most helpful. It is in this stage that each member's JOHARI window changes significantly. The JOHARI window is discussed in greater detail in chapter five. It is a representation of the intersection between what we know about and see in ourselves and what others know about and see in us. As we share information and participate in the group process, group members learn things about us that they may not have known before. As others share their perceptions of us we learn things about ourselves that we did not know before and are able to make adjustments in our attitudes and actions that we deem necessary and helpful to us. Group members invite the least involved members to participate more. The assigned leader's control fades. Leadership is shared by more group members although one or several members emerge as clear leaders of the group. The communication structure is completely decentralized. Members speak directly to one another in the second person "you," making eye contact and paying close attention to verbal and non-verbal cues. Roles become more diverse, as there is fuller participation by all group members. Power becomes even more distributed among all group members and more power bases are used. A power base is the source of one's ability to influence others in the group. Power is discussed in greater detail in chapter six.

STAGE FIVE: ENDING, DISENGAGEMENT, ADJOURNING, TERMINATION

During stage five, in sensitivity, counseling and therapy groups, interpersonal interactions become more complex as members have bonded and feel very connected to one another yet begin to realize that the group experience is coming to a close. The connections deepen on the one hand, but there is also a tendency to withhold additional deep sharing. Some members may

begin to withdraw and the level and quality of group participation may decline. Members may begin to feel a sense of impending loss and may bring
up past experiences of separation and loss, sharing how those experiences
affected them and drawing parallels with the impending separation from
the group. Members often begin to discuss ways that they may remain connected after the group terminates, thus forming friendship groups as spin-
offs from the present group. In groups such as work groups or on teams,
stage five may see an increase in activity and a redoubling of individual
and team efforts to meet deadlines and complete the product or deliverable
that is expected.

SHIFTS IN SHARING AND ENGAGEMENT

As the group evolves through the stages, the amount and quality of sharing and the depth of engagement among group members also change. In
stage one the sharing and engagement tend to be tentative and relatively
superficial. In stage two the sharing and engagement become more intense,
controversial, conflicting and genuine. In stage three, as trust develops
based on the attempts to resolve disagreements and conflicts in stage two,
the sharing and engagement tend to expand and deepen further. In stage
four as the group settles in and delves more deeply into the heart of its
work, sharing and engagement among group members tend to be at the
highest level. There is close to full and complete sharing and engagement
by all members of the group. In stage five, as termination approaches,
group members may begin to despair and withdraw. As a result, the level
of sharing and engagement among group members tend to decline except
perhaps in some work groups, when at this stage there may be a concerted
effort to complete the work and have a finished product to meet a deadline.
These shifts in sharing and engagement take the form of a bell curve as
shown in figure 2.1.

   Given the changes that occur in the group's dynamics as the group
moves from one stage to the other, it is possible to observe any group and
using a checklist to determine the stage that the group may be functioning
in at any point in time. Based on the Integrative Model of group development (Wheelan, 1994), a checklist has been developed specifically for this
purpose.

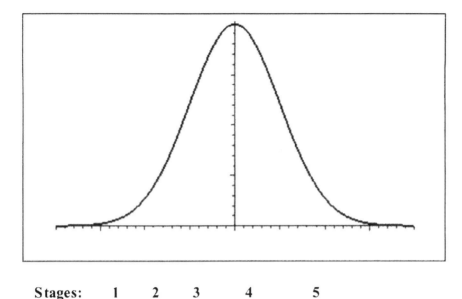

S tages: 1   2   3   4   5

Figure 2.1.   Sharing and Engagement among Group Members by Stages.

Stages of Group Development Checklist

Indicate the extent to which you agree or disagree with the following state-ments by using the following scale: Strongly Disagree =1, Disagree=2, Neu-tral=3, Agree=4 or Strongly Agree=5.

Activity # 2: Assessing Group Development—Observing a Film

In this activity each group member is required to view a film of a group in progress and, using the Stages of Group Development Checklist, indepen-dently score the group on the dimensions of each of the five stages. The stage on which the group scores the highest is the stage at which the group is as-sessed to be functioning. If there is a tie between two stages then the group is assessed to be transitioning from the earlier stage to the next stage. After assessing the observed group's stage of functioning, the observing group members share and discuss their assessments.

Table 2.2.

Stage One Indicators	Strongly Disagree =1	Disagree = 2	Neutral =3	Agree = 4	Strongly Agree = 5
The group members seem tentative and unsure.					
Communication is centralized and concentrated in the assigned leader.					
The group members look to the assigned leader for direction and guidance.					
The sharing and engagement among group members tends to be superficial.					
Group members are concerned with being accepted and included.					
There is little or no evidence of disagreement or conflict.					

Score:

Table 2.3.

Stage Two Indicators	Strongly Disagree =1	Disagree = 2	Neutral =3	Agree = 4	Strongly Agree = 5
The assigned leader is challenged.					
Communication is less centralized and more direct among group members.					
There is evidence of disagreements or conflict among group members.					
Subgroups or cliques are beginning to form.					
Clear roles among members are beginning to emerge.					
The level of sharing and engagement among group members is increasing in frequency and substance.					

Score:

Table 2.4.

Stage Three Indicators	Strongly Disagree =1	Disagree = 2	Neutral =3	Agree = 4	Strongly Agree = 5
There is increased trust among group members.					
Conflict resolution strategies are in place.					
Group members assume more group roles.					
There is a notable shift in leadership from the assigned leader, with group leadership emerging among group members.					
There is constructive feedback among members.					
Group members take more risks in sharing.					

Score:

Table 2.5.

Stage Four Indicators	Strongly Disagree =1	Disagree = 2	Neutral =3	Agree = 4	Strongly Agree = 5
Communication is completely decentralized.					
Conflict resolution strategies are used effectively to advance the work of the group.					
Group members share openly and confidently receiving and giving feedback to an almost equal degree with members. In doing so members are making eye contact and using the second person "you" more frequently.					
Group cohesion, connectedness and bonding are very evident.					
Group members experience significant personal growth.					
The work of the group gets accomplished.					

Score:

Table 2.6.

Stage Five Indicators	Strongly Disagree =1	Disagree = 2	Neutral =3	Agree = 4	Strongly Agree = 5
Group members begin to hold back on sharing new deep personal information.					
Group members talk more about their feelings and thoughts about the group ending.					
Group members reflect on past experiences with separation and loss.					
Group members make plans for maintaining connections after the group terminates.					
Group members disclose how they plan to use the information and skills they have acquired.					
Group members reflect on the effectiveness of the group in meeting stated goals and on the impact of the group experience on their personal growth.					

Score:

Activity # 3: Assessing Group Development—
Reflecting on Group Progress

In this activity each group member is required reflect on the group's progress at the end of each group session using the Stages of Group Development Checklist to independently score the group on the dimensions of each of the five stages as the group progresses over time. The assessment is to be used as part of reflective journaling that each group member does after each session. The stage on which the group scores the highest is the stage at which the group is assessed to be functioning at any point in time. If there is a tie between two stages then the group is assessed to be transitioning from the earlier stage to the next stage. The assessment of the group's stage of group development will be shared along with the group member's reflective journal at the beginning of the next group session.

Chapter Three

Steps in Forming a Group

In this chapter some important steps in forming a group are presented and discussed.

1. Determine and clearly articulate the purpose and goals of the group you are planning to form (what you would like the participants in the group to learn and achieve).
2. Determine the kind of group that would best address the purpose (counseling group, support group etc.).
3. Decide if you would like to have a closed or an open group.
4. Decide on the size of the group.
5. Decide how you would recruit participants for the group.
6. Select participants based on the goodness of fit between the goals of the group and the participants' needs and abilities to contribute to the group. You must use good clinical judgment and/ or use some form of screening mechanism.
7. Get written consent from participants or from parents or guardians of participants who are below the age of consent (18 years old).
8. Host the group in a private, comfortable and safe place.
9. During the first group session establish a sense of safety and trust by creating a welcoming climate. Use an icebreaking activity to relax and introduce/reintroduce participants and discuss and assure confidentiality.

STEP ONE: DETERMINE AND CLEARLY ARTICULATE THE PURPOSE AND GOALS OF THE GROUP YOU ARE PLANNING TO FORM.

As simple and as obvious as it may seem, the first step in forming a group, that is, identifying and stating the group's purpose and goals, is far too often overlooked or not given adequate attention. The purpose is a general statement about what the group is being formed to accomplish. The goals emanate from the purpose and are more specific statements about what the group is designed to achieve or what the indicators of group success would look like. Goals break down the purpose into more assessable units or outcomes. It is important to very clearly state the purpose of the group so that the goals can be clearly aligned with the purpose and the activities of the group can be aligned with the goals. The goals should be stated in measurable terms so that the progress of the group can be measured and monitored. Having goals allows the group designer and/or leader to assess the effectiveness of the group during and after the group process.

For example, assume that you are interested in forming a group to address a problem of overeating and under-activity among a group of overweight teenagers. The purpose of the group may be stated as: *to help the group of overweight teenagers consume fewer calories and become more active.* The goals may be stated as: to help the group of overweight teenagers: (1) eat fewer sweets, (2) drink fewer high calorie drinks, (3) snack less during the course of the day, (4) exercise for at least half an hour each day, and (5) reduce the amount of time sitting in front of a television or computer. In this example, the purpose is a general statement about fewer caloric consumption and higher levels of activity. The goals more specifically indicate measurable ways to achieve the group's purpose. Notice that the goals did not include any mention of weight loss because the purpose did not mention weight loss, although the ultimate aim is obviously weight loss. So for example, if the purpose is stated as: *to help overweight teenagers lose weight*, then the goals would be stated differently such as: to help overweight teenagers (1) monitor and manage their weight, (2) control their eating of foods that contribute to weight gain, (3) lose at least one pound each week, and (4) lose at least 10 pounds by the end of the group. As another example, assume that you are interested in forming a group for children of parents who are separated or divorced. The purpose of the group may be stated as: to help children of parents who are separated or divorced adjust well to the new family situation. The goals of th4e group can be stated as to help these children (1) recognize and express their emotional response to the change in their family situation,

(2) show that they understand that although each situation, such as their own, is different that they are not alone, (3) show that they understand that they are not responsible for their parents' problems, and (4) demonstrate that they accept the change in their family situation.

STEP TWO: DETERMINE THE KIND OF GROUP THAT WOULD BEST ADDRESS THE PURPOSE AND GOALS (COUNSELING GROUP, THERAPY GROUP, SUPPORT GROUP, WORK GROUP, FOCUS GROUP, PSYCHO-EDUCATIONAL OR SENSITIVITY GROUP).

The kind of group that is planned, designed and formed is determined by the purpose and the goals identified in step one. A counseling or therapy group, for example, would be appropriate to address goals that involve attitude and behavior change, life skills development and adjustment and adaptation to a changing situation. A support group would be appropriate to address goals that involve coping and acceptance. A work group would address goals that involve task completion. A focus group would address goals that involve data and information gathering on attitudes, preferences, perceptions and behavior. A sensitivity group would address goals that involve self-awareness, personal growth and interactions with others.

STEP THREE: DECIDE IF YOU WOULD LIKE TO HAVE A CLOSED OR AN OPEN GROUP.

The decision to form a closed or an open group would depend on the purpose, goals and kind of group. For example, most counseling groups are closed, that is, once the group begins no other individuals are allowed to join and those who have joined are expected to attend consistently. Most support groups are open. That is, there is no formal membership and individuals are allowed to attend as they wish. A good example is Alcoholics Anonymous.

STEP FOUR: DECIDE ON THE SIZE FOR THE GROUP.

The optimum size of a well-functioning and effective group ranges between 5-10 members. There are advantages and disadvantages in having a smaller sized group or a larger sized group. The smaller sized group has the advantage of greater involvement and participation by each member of the group.

However, it offers less diversity of the membership attributes including ideas and feedback. The larger sized group has the opposite advantage and disadvantage. With a larger membership, the advantage is that there is more likely to be more diversity among members. The disadvantage is that each member may participate less. The decision about size should be determined again by the purpose and goals of the group and is influenced by the kind of group that is being formed. For example, a counseling or therapy group may be usually smaller in size than a focus group or a support group. This is so because a counseling or therapy group is designed to produce change in members' attitudes or behaviors and requires a depth of personal commitment, involvement, sharing and feedback among group members that a focus group or support group may not require.

STEP FIVE: DECIDE HOW GROUP MEMBERS WOULD BE RECRUITED.

The methods used to recruit group members are important because how members are recruited determines who the members are and to a large extent the health and effectiveness of the group. Far too often the recruitment of group members is done haphazardly with insufficient attention paid to the goodness of fit between recruited members and the purpose and goals of the group. Not everyone who wants to participate in a group or is referred to a group is a good fit for that group. In fact the inclusion of some individuals in a group may endanger the group's viability, effectiveness and success. For example, in some instances, individuals with personality disorders or social and emotional problems should be excluded from participating in groups and may be better served in individual counseling or therapy sessions. In other instances, however, recruiting such individuals may be appropriate for therapy groups whose purpose is to address those personality disorders or social and emotional problems, with very experienced and skilled clinicians. Groups are not to be used as places where children with discipline problems are sent to free a classroom of disruptive children if the group is not designed for that purpose. Misuse of groups is a far too common problem that needs to be prevented, addressed and discontinued when identified. A screening interview and a screening checklist or questionnaire can be helpful in determining whether or not an individual is a good fit for a group. Below is an example of a screening checklist that may be used.

Using the checklist in table 3.1, an individual will be ruled out for group participation if that individual does not receive a check for each criterion or a score of 10 out of 10.

Table 3.1.

Criteria	Check	Comment
1. Is the appropriate age for the group		
2. Does not have a personality disorder that may impede the work of the group or limit the benefits of the group experience		
3. Does not have emotional problems that may impede the work of the group or limit the benefits of the group experience		
4. Does not have social problems that may impede the work of the group or limit the benefits of the group experience		
5. Does not have physical challenge that may impede the work of the group or limit the benefits of the group experience		
6. Is facing an issue that fits with the purpose and goals of the group		
7. Is willing and able to participate in group interactions including giving and receiving feedback		
8. Is willing to sign a group participation consent agreement or can have a consent agreement signed by a parent or guardian		
9. Is willing and able to attend the required number of group sessions		
10. Accepts and is willing to abide by all preconditions specified by the group facilitator		

STEP SIX: GET WRITTEN CONSENT FROM PARTICIPANTS OR FROM PARENTS OR GUARDIANS OF PARTICIPANTS WHO ARE BELOW THE AGE OF CONSENT (18 YEARS OLD).

A group facilitator should clearly explain the purpose and goals of the group and receive written consent from each group member before the group begins. This helps to ensure that each group member understands the group's purpose and goals and the responsibilities and expectations for group members. Below are examples of group participation consent and assent forms that can be used to document that group participation is done willingly.

CHILD'S GROUP PARTICIPATION PARENT OR GUARDIAN CONSENT FORM

I freely and willingly give consent for my child_____ to participate in the _____ Group that will be facilitated by _____. The purpose of the group is to_____ _____. The goals of the group are :_____

I understand that all information discussed or shared by participants in the group will be treated with strict confidentiality and that no information will be disclosed or shared with others outside of the group except when absolutely necessary to protect the safety of group participants, including myself, or others, or if mandated by a court of law. I understand that I am free to withdraw this consent at any time that I may choose.

_____   _____

Signature of Participant's Parent or Guardian   Date

ADULT GROUP PARTICIPATION ASSENT FORM

I freely and willingly consent to participate in the _____ Group that will be facilitated by _____. The purpose of the group is to_____. The goals of the group are:_____

_____

_____ I understand that all information discussed or shared by participants in the group will be treated with strict confidentiality and that no information will be disclosed or shared with others outside of the group except when absolutely necessary to protect the safety of group participants including myself, or others, or if mandated by a court of law. I understand that I am free to withdraw this consent at any time that I may choose.

_____   _____

Signature of Participant   Date

STEP SEVEN: HOST THE GROUP IN A PRIVATE, COMFORTABLE AND SAFE PLACE.

The location that is selected for hosting group sessions is just as important as the other steps discussed above. Location can impact group members' comfort level, feelings of safety and security, sense of confidentiality and privacy, and their willingness and motivation to fully engage in the group process. In some cases, such as in some schools, space limitations impose a challenging situation in finding an appropriate space to host groups. Careful negotiations to identify a space that meets the following criteria should be conducted with the school principal or person in charge of assigning space for such activities. An appropriate space for groups should be:

- private,
- protective of confidentiality,

- comfortable in terms of temperature, furniture, and lighting,
- arranged in a manner that facilitates eye contact among all group participants and free flowing communication and interaction,
- available on a regularly scheduled basis at a specified time,
- free from interruptions or disruptions by human traffic or noise from various sources,
- accessible to all group members.

Some time ago two group co-leaders wanted to facilitate a group in a middle school. There was some difficulty in identifying an appropriate space. The principal offered his office as a place to host the group. After the first two sessions the location had to be moved to a corner of the media center. The principal's phone rang constantly. There were frequent knocks on the door and the principal himself was in and out several times during the time the group was being held. The change in location went relatively smoothly but the disruption and location change had a noticeable impact on the comfort level of group members and the dynamics of the group.

STEP EIGHT: ESTABLISH A SENSE OF SAFETY AND TRUST DURING THE FIRST SESSION BY CREATING A WELCOMING CLIMATE, AND REINFORCE THIS CLIMATE DURING SUBSEQUENT SESSIONS.

When a group is formed, a new experience begins for all members of the group. During the first session members tend to be uncertain, anxious, lacking confidence that they may do or say the right things and depend on the assigned leader for direction and guidance and to derive a sense of inclusion. Using an icebreaking activity to relax and introduce/reintroduce participants and discuss and assure confidentiality, can be extremely helpful and is highly recommended. As the name suggests, icebreaking activities break the ice, reduce the feeling of coldness or coolness that group members may be experiencing, and create warmth and establish comfort. Icebreaking activities with specific examples are further discussed in chapter five.

Activity # 4: Forming a Group in a School

You are working in a school as a specialist in your field. You discover that there are students in your school who can benefit from group counseling services. You consult with the principal who gives you the go ahead to offer group counseling to students. Please identify an issue based on your interest, knowledge or experience for which students may need counseling services. Follow the eight steps above and discuss how you would go about establishing a counseling group.

Or

Activity # 5: Forming a Group in a Mental Health Setting

You are working in a mental health facility as a specialist in your field. You discover that there are clients in your facility who can benefit from group counseling services. You consult with your supervisor who gives you the go ahead to offer group counseling to clients. Please identify an issue based on your interest, knowledge or experience for which clients may need counseling services. Follow the eight steps above and discuss how you would go about establishing a counseling group.

Chapter Four

Selected Essential Elements of Group Culture and Structure

GROUP NORMS

Norms are guidelines that govern the manner in which group members interact with one another during the group process. They serve as expected standards of behavior among group members. Norms may also guide how members talk to others outside of the group about what goes on in the group. For example, respecting the confidentiality of information shared within the group and not disclosing such information to others outside of the group is a universally accepted group norm. In children's groups, norms may be referred to as rules. For example, in a children's group a rule might be that a group member should raise his or her hand to be acknowledged before speaking. Another rule might be that group members should not leave the group without the expressed approval of the group leader. Norms may be explicit or implicit. *Explicit norms* are those that are openly expressed, discussed and written. *Implicit norms* are those that evolve during the group process and are inherently understood by group members to be accepted ways of behaving and interacting within the group. Implicit norms may not be written or verbalized, but are expressed in the manner in which group members intuitively interact. For example, an explicit norm might be that group members respect the confidentiality of all information shared during the group process. An example of an implicit norm might be that group members make eye contact with other members when addressing them.

Many norms are generated by members of the group. Other norms may be predetermined and introduced by the group facilitator as preconditions for the effective functioning of the group. As much as possible, it is important for the group facilitator to allow group members to generate their own norms. When group members generate the group norms there tends to be more commitment and greater adherence to these norms. In children's groups, more so than in adult groups, there is a tendency for group members to want to impose tangible penalties for violation of group norms. However, it is important for the group facilitator to confront (point out) group members' violations of group norms and to invite feedback from other group members regarding norm violations.

Norms may be generated in several ways. One way is to simply ask group members to brainstorm norms for consideration by the group. Members express what they believe the norms should be. Each idea is written down on a smart board, white board or flip chart as it is presented. When all of the ideas are written, each one is discussed and considered by the group for inclusion or exclusion. A final list of norms is then agreed to and each norm on the list becomes an explicit norm. Another approach to establishing norms is to make three columns on a smart board, white board or flip chart. The first column includes what group members would like to get from the group. The second column includes what group members are willing to give to the group to get what they want. The group then goes through each column to remove redundancies and to discuss each item. The third column then includes items from the first two columns that members of the group agree on that can be adopted as group norms. This approach may take longer than the first, but it allows for more sharing, discussion and feedback while establishing group norms. Both approaches can also serve as icebreakers.

Below is an example of norms determined by the professor of an experiential group dynamics class in which group/class members learned about the basic principles of group dynamics, while actually being a group and observing and studying themselves as a group.

- Attend All Class-Group Meetings
- Be Punctual
- Respect and Honor Confidentiality
- Have Open Minds
- Respect Members
- Be Non-Judgmental
- Practice Active Listening
- Practice Honest Sharing of Feelings, Thoughts and Ideas
- Be Willing to Express Conflicting Opinions, Ideas and Feelings
- Be Aware of Verbal and Non-Verbal Messages Among Group Members

Below is an example of norms generated and identified by the class-group:

Explicit: These are norms that the group and the professor decided on during the first session:

- Attend Every Session
- Participate Fully
- Respect Confidentiality
- Participate Fully in the Group Project
- Complete the Exam
- Always Be Prepared (book, pen, paper)
- Implicit: These are norms that the group reported emerged over time.
- Be Respectful
- Listen Actively
- Be Supportive
- Share Honestly
- Be Polite

GROUP ROLES

Group members assume various roles during the group process. Group roles significantly influence group dynamics. Each role that a group member plays contributes to the dynamics of the group, enriches the group process and benefits group members. Roles are classified into three major categories: *task roles, group building and maintenance roles and individual roles.*

Task Roles: These are roles that contribute to the advancement of the work of the group and help the group accomplish its tasks. They are presented in alphabetical order below:

- *Coordinator:* The coordinator organizes the group's ideas and suggestions and orchestrates the group's work.
- *Elaborator:* The elaborator expands on and explains ideas and suggestions offered by members of the group.
- *Energizer:* The energizer motivates the group to keep working and to get things done.
- *Evaluator/Critic:* The evaluator/critic considers and refers the group members to the purpose, goals and norms in critiquing and assessing the group's progress and accomplishments.
- *Information Giver:* The information giver offers factual information based on knowledge and experience.

- *Information Seeker*: The information seeker requests information to clarify ideas or suggestions and to check on factual accuracy.
- *Initiator/Contributor:* The initiator/contributor suggests or proposes new ideas to the group.
- *Opinion Giver:* The opinion giver offers thoughts and beliefs about suggestions and ideas shared within the group.
- *Opinion Seeker:* The opinion seeker tries to get opinions from other group members on topics, ideas and suggestions in order to clarify group members' positions and values.
- *Orienter:* The orienter summarizes the group's process and monitors, calibrates and defines the progress of the group.
- *Procedural Technician:* The procedural technician performs logistical and routine tasks to support and expedite the group's work.
- *Recorder:* The recorder keeps track of decisions and suggestions by writing or typing notes and by keeping a running record of the group's work.

Group Building and Maintenance Roles: These are roles that contribute to the cohesion and bonding that occur within the group. They are presented in alphabetical order below:

- *Compromiser*: The compromiser gives up some of his or her held views and ideas in a compromising way in order to arrive at a mutually agreeable position or agreement on issues.
- *Encourager*: The encourager validates, reinforces, supports, commends, recognizes and values contributions from group members.
- *Follower:* The follower goes along in a passive and uncritical way with any suggestions, ideas, decisions or activities proposed or advanced by other group members.
- *Gatekeeper/Expediter:* The gatekeeper/expediter monitors, solicits and supports input by group members and encourages group discussion and communication.
- *Harmonizer:* The harmonizer mediates and reconciles disagreements, disputes and conflict among group members.
- *Observer/Commentator:* The observer/ commentator conducts critical observations of the group's work and comments on the group's process.
- *Standard Setter:* The standard setter establishes and applies criteria for evaluating the group's process and progress.

Individual Roles: These are roles that meet idiosyncratic needs of individual group members within the group. By taking on any one or any combination of these roles the individual is seeking to satisfy a personal need and using the group to do so. The individual roles are presented in alphabetical order below

- *Aggressor:* The aggressor tends to attack members of the group and the group as a whole and takes credit for the ideas and suggestions of others.
- *Arguer:* The arguer persistently disagrees with the opinions and ideas of others in the group and the views of the group as a whole. In doing so the arguer seeks to satisfy a personal need to assert him or herself and to be contrary to the group's consensus positions.
- *Blocker:* The blocker seeks to impede the work and progress of the group or stop certain activities or processes in the group by being negative, disagreeable and resistant.
- *Dominator:* The dominator imposes authority and control and asserts superiority over other members of the group through manipulation.
- *Player:* The player ostensibly displays a lack of interest and involvement in the group to draw attention.
- *Recognition Seeker:* The recognition seeker attempts to draw attention to him or herself by using various means and methods.
- *Self-Confessor:* The self-confessor cathartically shares and expresses personal problems and feelings to such an extent that limits the input of other group members. This role may include elements of the other individual roles and may serve similar functions.

All of the roles identified above contribute to the overall group's dynamics and may be considered to be important to the group's work and process. It can be easy to see the individual roles as perhaps unhealthy for the group as a whole, when in fact this may not be so. One has to keep in mind that many groups are formed in part or in whole to help the individual grow, resolve personal issues and to achieve a sense of belonging and purpose. When a group member takes on any of the individual roles, the group may in fact be doing its work.

Activity # 6: Group Member Roles

It is helpful to be able to identify and reflect on the different roles that group members play in the group. In tables 4.1, 4.2 and 4.3 are three grids that can be used to do this. On the vertical axis of each grid are listed the roles that members play. On the horizontal axis of each grid are blank spaces for the names or initials of group members. One way to use each grid is to place a check mark in each box where the role and a member's name or initials intersect when a member is observed to have played that role. Another approach

Table 4.1.   Task Roles Checklist.

Names or Initials/ Roles Played

Coordinator
Elaborator
Energizer
Evaluator/Critic
Information Giver
Information Seeker
Initiator/Contributor
Opinion Giver
Opinion Seeker
Orienter
Procedural Technician
Recorder
Comments:

Table 4.2.   Group Building and Maintenance Roles.

Names or Initials/ Roles Played

Compromiser
Encourager
Follower
Gatekeeper and Expediter
Harmonizer
Observer/Commentator
Standard Setter
Comments:

Table 4.3.   Individual Roles Checklist.

Names or Initials/ Roles Played

Aggressor
Arguer
Blocker
Dominator
Player
Recognition Seeker
Self-Confessor
Comments:

is to write members' name or initials in the boxes next to the roles that they are observed to have played. The result is the same with both approaches. The grids are then used to provide direct and specific feedback among group members.

Activity # 7: Perceived, Actual and Expected Role

This activity can also be used as a self-reflective activity by group members to reflect on the roles they believe they have played during a group session or are usually playing in the group. The individual checks off the roles that he or she thinks that he or she is playing. He or she may then solicit feedback from the group on his or her *perceived role*. The group may then provide direct feedback on the member's *actual or enacted role* and what the role the group expected the individual to play which is referred to as the *expected role*. When the perceived role, enacted role and expected role are not in sync or are not consistent, *role ambiguity* or *role confusion* is said to occur. Role ambiguity is believed to lead to a group member's lowered self-esteem and satisfaction and lowered group morale. When a group member plays incompatible or contradictory roles in a group then *role conflict* is said to occur. This can be unsettling to individuals and they may try to minimize role conflict by assuming non-contradictory positions in groups

GROUP CLIMATE AND LEADERSHIP AND CLIMATE

The group's *climate* refers to the social-emotional and psychological atmosphere that prevails in the group. A group's climate is often tied to the style of leadership that the group's leader or facilitator practices in the group. A group's climate is often classified in one of two major ways: *(1) group-centered or leader-centered or (2) autocratic, democratic or laissez faire.* Groups that are considered group-centered tend to have the characteristics identified with democratic leadership. Groups that are considered to be leader-centered tend to have characteristics that are associated with autocratic leadership. Groups that are considered to be laissez-faire seem to have no clear leadership or structured organization. These are further discussed below.

Group-Centered and Leader-Centered Groups

In groups with a *group-centered climate*, group members set the tone and drive the group's dynamics. Their views, opinions, ideas and suggestions, feelings, perspectives, and perceptions are respected, valued, validated and recognized by the group leader and by one another. There tends to be strong commitment to the group process among group members, more buy-in to the group's tasks and more shared responsibility among group members. Members tend to show stronger adherence to the norms of the group and tend to identify more strongly with the group than they do in non-group-centered groups. In *leader-centered climate* groups, the leader tends to control the process and group members tend to orient their behavior and participation toward the leader rather than to one another. There may be more uncertainty, tentativeness, lack of commitment to group norms, and dissatisfaction among group members. It may be argued that for most, if not for all groups, during stage one of a group's development the group is likely to have a leader-centered climate and as the group development progresses it may become more group-centered.

Autocratic, Democratic and Laissez Faire Groups

In groups with an *autocratic climate*, the leader tends to be aloof from group members, takes control of setting the norms, methods and tone of the group and, in general, seeks to instill and impose his or her values on the group. It may be argued that in certain situations this kind of group leadership and group climate are expected, warranted and may lead to desired outcomes. The military is sometimes cited as an example of group situations where autocratic leadership is practiced. In the military, an autocratic group climate prevails and leads to the desired results, which are strict discipline and a high degree of conformity among the rank and file. However, the abundance of evidence in counseling literature supports the notion that a non-autocratic climate better serves the interests of group members and the overall purpose of the group.

In groups with a *democratic climate* there is open and direct communication among group members as well as shared leadership. The assigned leader actively seeks to involve group members in offering suggestions and ideas while praising and encouraging group participation. Each group member feels that he or she is respected, accepted, valued and an important member of the group. The group norms are established together and there are clear expectations for group participation and standards for group interactions. Group members are highly motivated to participate and are driven by their individual and collective desire to see the group succeed. Most, if not all counseling, therapy, sensitivity and other therapeutic and support groups tend to have a democratic climate.

In groups with a *laissez-faire climate*, the assigned leader, as in the autocratic group tends to be aloof, however, the difference is that in the autocratic group the leader is very much engaged and takes full and total control. In the Laissez-faire group the leader's aloofness is tantamount to disengagement and abandonment of leadership responsibility. There is no clear leadership either individual or collective. There tends to be a lack of clear norms, expectations and standards for interactions and behavior in the group. It is as if anything goes. The group may seem chaotic, disorganized and direction-less. Some sensitivity groups may begin with a laissez-faire climate in order to organically produce leadership, norms and standards and then evolve to democratic groups.

Activity #8: Group Process

Students will watch a film of a group process and individually fill in the grid in table 4.4 by placing a check mark in the box that best describes each observed group process characteristic in the rows. Check democratic, auto-

Table 4.4.

Group Climate/ Group Process Characteristics	Democratic: Occurs in an Organized and Coherent Way and Influenced and Organized by Group Members'	Autocratic Totally Controlled by Assigned Leader With Little or No Influence by Group Members	Laissez-Faire Occurs in a Disorganized and Almost Chaotic Fashion
Group Leadership			
Group Norms			
Group Members' Participation			
Group Members' Feelings of Acceptance and Being valued			
Group Members' Expressions of Satisfaction or Dissatisfaction			
Group's Sense of Direction and Purpose			
Group Members' Adherence to Norms			
Communication Within the Group			
Decision Making			
Feedback			
Comments:			

cratic or laissez-faire. The column with the most checks indicates the kind of climate in the observed group. Each student will then discuss his or her rating of the group process with other members in his or her small group.

GROUP CONFORMITY

Conformity to group norms is indicative of commitment and dedication to the group's process and progress. Norms help to bring about group cohesion, bonding, and identity and, to some extent, control. Members who do not conform to the group norms and expectations act in direct conflict to group values. Members who desire group acceptance, affiliation and connection to the group tend to conform. Members who follow group norms faithfully are called *conformists*. In conforming, they avoid the negative consequences of rejection and ostracism or whatever other sanctions the group may impose. Some group members move continually between conforming to group norms and not conforming or violating group norms. These members are referred to as *sliders*. Other group members defy and violate group norms continually and do not fear or shy away from retribution in the form of rejection, ostracism or imposition of sanctions by the group. They are referred to as *non-conformists*. Sliders and non-conformists may be seeking to satisfy individual needs inherent in any one of the individual roles discussed earlier in this chapter.

GROUP THINK

Group think is related to group conformity. It occurs when group members relinquish their beliefs, critical and evaluative thinking and their standards of conduct and think only in concert with the group's values, beliefs and standards. Group think may be seen as an extreme form of group conformity. There are three major factors that inspire group think. These are: *unrealistic beliefs about the group's power, close-mindedness and pressure to agree.*

Unrealistic Beliefs about the Group's Power: Group members may come to believe that because of the power of the group they are invincible. They internalize the mistaken notion that the group's collective power can protect and shield them from any threat, retaliation or retribution. As a result, group members may be convinced to take extreme risks. They may tend to do risky things when they are with members of the group that they may not do when they are alone. This phenomenon is called *risky shift.* It is a shift in the level and degree of risk that the group member is willing to take because of the unrealistic belief in the group's power. Gang members, for example, are willing to commit extremely terrible acts without regard to the consequences, that as individuals they may not do, because of their allegiance to and belief in the power of the gang. Fraternity and sorority members take risks when with their fraternity brothers and sorority sisters that, as individuals, they may not take. Soldiers on the battlefield perform acts of bravery and heroism that, as individuals, they may not perform. Bullies are usually surrounded by other bullies or supporters and may not bully if alone.

Close-Mindedness: Group members may disregard and discount warnings and indications of negative outcomes or adverse consequences of acting in a certain way. There seems to be a quality of single-mindedness about following through on an action sanctioned by the group regardless of information that should cause group members to rethink, reconsider and revise their actions. In situations when someone else outside of the group is being victimized as a result of group think, the tendency is to rationalize behavior, and if necessary, vilify and stereotype the perceived enemy to justify actions against the victim. For example, in the situation in which a group of students may bully another student, they may disregard the possibility of suspension and/ or expulsion from school and may justify their actions by labeling the bullied student in ways that may suggest that the victim invited or deserved the negative treatment.

Pressure to Agree: The group demands loyalty from members and does not tolerate dissent. Group members apply pressure to other group members to conform to the group's norms and expectations when such members appear to be drifting away from the group's expected ways of thinking and behaving. Members yield to the group's pressure to gain acceptance and favor with the group and to avoid rejection and ostracism by the group. Group members who have high affiliation needs are most vulnerable to this pressure by the group to conform.

While "*group think*" is often viewed as a negative phenomenon because it is frequently associated with group coercion to do undesirable things or think in undesirable ways, group think sometimes can be positive and can result in desirable outcomes. The three major factors to conform apply to the positive view of "group think" just as they apply to the negative view. For example, a child or teenager who is unmotivated and underachieving in school, but who wishes to join the basketball or hockey team (a team is a group), may be granted membership only if he or she conforms to the academic standards set by the team. In the child's or teenager's mind, the requirement to meet the high academic standards while practicing enough to win may seem unrealistic (unrealistic beliefs about the group's power). The child or teenager may protest and complain about fatigue and stress but the team may continue to insist on very high academic performance (close-mindedness). The team may strengthen its resolve to promote each player as a scholar athlete and may institute a policy of receiving and reviewing on-going teacher progress reports for each team member, penalizing each team member who falls below a certain grade cut off (pressure to agree). Another example may be a social club whose primary mission is to help the homeless through volunteer activities. Someone wishing to be a member of this group may be required to accept certain positive standards of behavior to become and remain a member of this group. The volunteer group may set a goal of feeding, clothing and housing at least fifty homeless families a quarter (unrealistic beliefs about the group's power). The group may ignore evidence suggesting the cost of meeting its quarterly goals may far exceed its budget or capacity to raise the funds (close-mindedness). When a member of the group suggests that the goals be scaled back, the group counters by suggesting that the member may not be as committed to the project as she should be. Further, the group may propose that she may be a hindrance rather than an asset to the group's effort if she continues to raise objections (pressure to agree). These two examples are positive examples of *group think* because all members are expected to act in agreement with the values of the groups and the groups would not tolerate any deviation from the positive values and expectations they espouse.

Activity #9: Positive and Negative Group Think

Write two scripts for two vignettes, one vignette demonstrating the more usual negative interpretation of *group think* and the other demonstrating the less usual positive interpretation of *group think*. For each script, include and explain the three factors underlying group think: unrealistic beliefs about the group's power, close-mindedness, and pressure to agree. Act out the vignettes.

GROUP COMMUNICATION STRUCTURE

Communication structures in groups can range along a continuum from *centralized* to *decentralized*. Highly centralized communication structures are those in which the communication among members of a group or organization is strictly controlled and distributed by a central figure or authority. In very complex organizations one tends to see hierarchical models of management, and with that, there tends to be highly centralized communication structures, For example, presented in figure 4.1 is a hierarchical structure in which workers in lower level positions communicate with supervisors who communicate with a mid-level manager who communicates with senior level managers who communicate with the Chief Operating Officer (COO). This highly centralized organization/communication structure may look like that shown in figure 4.1.

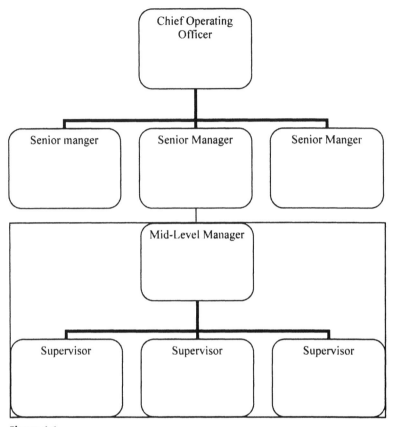

Figure 4.1.

Highly decentralized communication structures are those in which communication among members is free flowing, direct, unimpeded and uncensored. This structure is often represented by a circle as shown in figure 4.2.

Between these two extremes there is a continuum of communication structures with varying degrees of control and openness. Leavitt (1951) studied five person groups and suggested a continuum of communication structures from centralized to decentralized. Four examples of communication structures are presented below ranging from the Wheel which is highly centralized to the circle which is highly decentralized. The diagrams in figures 4.3 and 4.4 taken from Borgatti (1996) depict the centralized and decentralized structures.

Figure 4.2.

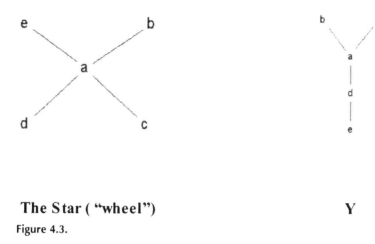

The Star ("wheel")   **Y**

Figure 4.3.

Centralized Communication Structures

In centralized communication structures information is filtered through and to some degree controlled by a central communications authority. These structures are best for addressing simple problems that can be done quickly. However, due to the control mechanisms in place usually with one person or few people being the central authority overload, bottleneck and inefficiency in decision-making can occur. Centralized communication structures are often classified into three categories: *the wheel structure, the Y structure and the chain structure.*

The Wheel

In the wheel structure there is a central authority, a person, group or department that controls or manages the information. For example, in some situations

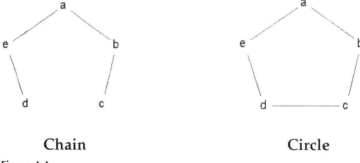

Chain   **Circle**

Figure 4.4.

as with the police department or the fire department, the central dispatchers receive emergency calls and manage this information by relaying it to officers or fire fighters in various locations. This kind of structure is often effective in managing the distribution of information in emergency situations. In the example of the wheel above, dispatcher "a" receives emergency calls and distributes the information to police officers "b," "c," "d" and "e" so that they may respond immediately.

The Y

In the Y structure there is a central authority, a person, group or department that controls, manages and distributes the information to one other entity or individual who then passes information on to others. For example, in some academic institutions, the President may pass on information to the Vice President of Academic Affairs, who then may pass information on to the Dean of the School of Education , who then may pass information on to various Department Chairs in that School. This kind of structure is often effective in managing the orderly and appropriate flow of information. Notice that the difference between this "Y" structure and the "wheel" structure is that there are more people managing the flow and distribution of information therefore, the information is less centralized. In the example of the "Y" structure above, "e" (the President) passes information to "d" (the Vice President of Academic Affairs) who in turn passes this information to "a" (the Dean of the School of Education) who then passes this information to "c" and "d" (the Department Heads within the School of Education).

The Chain

In the chain structure there is a central authority, either a person, group or department that controls, manages and distributes information to more than one other entity or individual who then pass information on to others. For example, in a mental health clinic, the clinical director may pass information on to more than one clinical care coordinators who then pass that information on to several case managers. This kind of structure is also effective in managing the orderly and appropriate flow of information. Notice that the difference between this "wheel" structure and the "chain" structure is that there are even more people managing the flow and distribution of information, therefore, the information is even less centralized or more decentralized. In the example of the "Y" structure above, "a" (clinical director) passes information to "b" and "e" (the clinical care coordinators) who in turn pass this information to "d" and "c" (case managers).

Decentralized Communication Structure

The Circle

In this decentralized structure, there is a free and unimpeded flow of information. All members of the group communicate directly and openly with one another. No one authority controls, manages and distributes the information. The information is generally passed around to all party members. When problem solving, these structures tend to work best for more complex problems.

In examining the relative strengths and weaknesses of centralized and decentralized communication structures when it comes to interfacing and problem solving, Borgatti (1996) noted that in the centralized structures, the number of possible patterns of communication was much smaller than in decentralized structures, thus limiting the number of ideas. In groups and on teams, members tend to feel forced to adopt a certain strategy for solving the problem. However, with the circle structure, there are many more ideas and suggestions proposed even though only a few may prove to be viable. Also, given the array of possible solutions proposed, it is sometimes more difficult for group or team members to select a strategy and follow through with it. Borgatti, (1997) noted:

> It is often the case in organizations that a satisfactory strategy that is easy to find, implement and stick to is superior to an optimal strategy that is hard to find, hard to implement, and hard to stick with.
>
> It is also helpful if the strategy that a structure pushes people towards is one that people are naturally positively disposed towards. For example, people readily understand leadership. It is much harder to understand the system which, in the circle, would actually lead to much faster performance than the integrator strategy.
>
> This strategy of choosing a satisfactory rather than optimal solution is known as satisficing, and is an important concept in organizational theory. It is part of a larger conception of organizations as systems that overcome human cognitive limitations—a condition known as bounded rationality. The idea of bounded rationality is that people are intendedly rational, but they can't really be rational because they can't consider all the possibilities. There isn't enough time, or information, nor the brains needed to sort it all out.

(http://www.analytictech.com/mb021/commstruc.htm)

Activity #10: Plotting Communication Patterns

This activity is designed to increase sensitivity and awareness of the communication structures of various groups of which an individual is a member.

Directions:

1. Select two significant groups of which you are a member.
2. Plot (draw a diagram) the communication pattern of each of the selected groups.
3. Compare the communication structures of the two groups. Discuss how they are similar and different
4. Identify your position and role in the communication structure of each group.
5. Describe and discuss how you feel about your position and role in the communication structure of each group.
6. Describe and discuss how you would change, if you could, the communication structure of each group and your position and role in each communication structure.

Activity #11: Communication Fish Bowl

Directions:

1. The group is divided into small groups of no more than five individuals.
2. One small group moves to the center forming an inner circle and is encircled by the remaining members of the larger group.
3. The members of the small inner group go through Activity # 10 above, plotting and discussing the communication structures of two selected groups, touching on each of the six points in the directions in Activity #10.
4. Members in the outer group, who serve as observers, monitor and document the interactions among members in the inner circle during the activity.
5. At the end of the sharing and discussions among members of the inner circle, the members of the outer group share their observations, ask questions and provide feedback about the communication structure and the varying roles that the inner group displayed while discussing Activity # 10.
6. The groups then trade places.

Chapter Five

Selected Essential Elements of the Group Process

While every group session is important and the value of each session needs to be fully realized, there is no doubt that the first group session sets the stage for the other sessions to follow. As such, the first session needs to be carefully facilitated so that all group members at the very beginning of the group process, stage one of the group's development, derive a sense of comfort, acceptance and value. As noted in chapter two, members in stage one tend to be uncertain, diffident, unconfident and seek a sense of inclusion, relying heavily on the group leader or facilitator for direction and connection. It is important, therefore, for the group facilitator to establish a climate of trust, comfort and confidentiality and to very clearly articulate the group's purpose, goals and the expectations of all group members. Some group leaders may have prepared contracts during the first session for members to read and to sign, while others may do this before the group begins in a pre-group meeting. It is also important and helpful in the first session for the group facilitator to state or reiterate and discuss the group's respect for the confidentiality of information that group members may share. The brainstorming of norms for the group during the first session may also help to establish a feeling of inclusion, empowerment and safety among group members.

Some groups may be single session groups or may be open groups for the participants of which, the first session they attend, may be the only one they will attend, or one of few they may irregularly attend. In these instances, the first session attended by the group participant may take on a different significance and meaning than the first session in a closed group that lasts for several regularly scheduled and consistent sessions. In cases of single session groups and open groups, each session should be carefully facilitated to make each member feel welcome, supported and comfortable. The session should also address the purpose for which the group is formed. Thus, the process for these groups, because of their nature, would require that the stages of development of the group proceed or evolve in a much more condensed period of time. The session must not only set the stage for a safe and comfortable level of sharing, but the work of the group must also be accomplished in this one session.

Subsequent sessions of a group that is a multiple session group should be sessions that move the group through each of the developmental stages toward accomplishing the group's purpose and goals before termination. Consequently, every session is to be facilitated with the utmost skill and sensitivity by the group facilitator, allowing each group member to participate fully and in a way that contributes to the group's vitality, meaningfulness, and productivity. The group process factors which are discussed below are essential to the effectiveness of the group.

ICEBREAKERS

During the first session and during subsequent sessions as needed, using icebreakers is an effective way to help address the anxiety and uncertainty that members may feel. Icebreakers are activities that get group members interacting and involved with one another in a safe, non-judgmental and non-threatening way. The first ice-breaker should probably be kept to a relatively easy and fairly surface level, of low to moderate cognitive and emotional challenge. It should not require group members to share too much deep personal information at this stage. The purpose is to get group members talking and comfortable with one another. A variety of icebreakers are available from many sources on the internet and in books. One icebreaker that this writer developed and has used is called: Find Someone Who, Part I. It is provided below.

Activity #12: Find Someone Who, Part I

Directions:

Group members are given a sheet of paper with 10 statements. Each group member is then invited to move around the room and to find one other individual in the group whose complete name, that is, first, middle and last name, he or she can write on the line next to each statement on the sheet. Each member is encouraged to find as many different members in the group as possible whose name can be written next to a statement. However, it is acceptable to write the same person's name for no more than two statements. After writing down the individual's name, each member then spends two to three minutes talking to the individual about the item or topic covered by the statement. This activity should take between 30 to 45 minutes depending on the size of the group. When the group convenes for processing, the activity is processed in terms of the "process" of the activity and the "content" that was shared during the activity. Processing the "process" examines how the activity unfolded; how group members began the activity and how they proceeded to fill in the names next to the items. It examines the approach to the activity. Processing the Content examines what was shared in response to the items. The content helps to establish linkages and connections among group members.

Find someone who:

Has the same number of siblings as you.
Shares a common ethnic or cultural heritage as you.
Has a pet.
Lives within five miles of you.
Has changed careers at least once.
Is a parent, uncle, aunt or grandparent.
Shares a similar hobby as you.
Was born during the same month as you.
Has travelled to or lived in another State or foreign country similar to you.
Has a favorite song, poem, book or painting similar to yours.

In this activity the content is light, non-threatening and should not provoke defensiveness or anxiety. It also includes topics that members in this early stage of the group may enjoy sharing and talking about. Additionally, it allows group members to meet and greet one another, get to know one another by name, and share aspects of themselves that can set the stage for forming deeper connections, bonding more and developing mutual trust.

ACTIVE LISTENING

Listening is not the same as hearing. Individuals can hear what someone else says without listening. The difference between listening and hearing is that the listener pays attention to the speaker and what the speaker says, so that what is heard is processed and digested in a meaningful way. Listening requires attention, focus and conscious processing of the information being heard. Hearing does not. Active listening is different from just listening or from passive listening, including all of the elements of passive listening and more. With active listening, the speaker feels and knows that he or she is being listened to by the verbal and non-verbal actions of the listener.

In counseling, the counselor is encouraged to listen actively and to demonstrate active listening by using what are called *minimal encouragers,* such as eye direct and focused contact, appropriate nodding of the head, appropriate changes in body posture to mirror the client's own posture, slight vocalizations such as "umm hmm," and appropriate facial expressions. Additionally, the active listener asks for clarification, paraphrases and summarizes what was said. When group members use active listening during the group process, the member who is listened to knows it, sees it, feels it and feels connected, valued and important.

Activity #13: Active Listening

Directions:

1. Group members are divided into triads.
2. Each member is given a numbered card with a role identified on the card. There are three numbered roles. Role #1 is the member sharing a very important personal experience. Role #2 is the member actively listening. Role #3 is the member hearing but not listening and engaging in overt inattentive behaviors. Roles # 2 and # 3 are kept secret from the person with role #1.
3. After 10 minutes of sharing, the member with Role #1 guesses who the active listener was and who was not and discusses how he or she felt about the behaviors of the other two members of the triad.
4. After 15 minutes the cards are exchanged among members in each triad and then the members with role # 1 and role # 3 cards rotate by moving to different triads. The process is repeated until each member in the group gets to assume each of the three roles in a triad. The discussion of each role should take about 15 minutes. The whole activity should take about 45 minutes. Does Role #1 discuss how he or she felt for 15 minutes or does the whole.
5. The activity is then processed in the larger group in terms of the process and the content that was shared.

DEFENSE MECHANISMS

During the group process, particularly during therapeutic, sensitivity and support groups, some members use a variety of defense mechanisms to protect themselves from criticism by others or from being judged in a negative way. Defense mechanisms are unconscious ways that the ego finds to protect itself. The ego is that part of the conscious self that is protective of one's sense of self-worth and self-esteem. To some degree defense mechanisms may work to protect the individual, but when overused defensive mechanisms can lead to maladaptive ways of thinking and behaving. Some of the most common defense mechanisms include the following:

- *Denial*: Insistence that one has not done or said something or does not feel a certain way.
- *Rationalization*: Advancing a reason for a behavior that appears plausible.
- *Reaction Formation*: Acting in a way that is completely opposite to the way one really feels about a situation or toward someone.
- *Sublimation*: Finding a socially acceptable way to express a socially unacceptable desire
- *Repression*: Keeping from consciousness an unpleasant or disturbing experience.
- *Regression*: Psychologically and/or emotionally returning to an earlier developmental stage.

GIVING AND RECEIVING FEEDBACK

The giving and receiving of feedback among group members throughout the group process is an indispensable process feature of most groups, especially counseling and therapy groups, sensitivity groups and support groups. When a group member gives feedback he or she reveals information about him or herself to others in the group that they may not have known before. When a group member receives feedback, he or she comes to know more about how he or she is being perceived by others. The giving and receiving of feedback also helps to cut through defense mechanisms that may be getting in the way of personal growth and progress. As a result, group members grow cognitively and emotionally from giving and receiving feedback. They learn things about other members and about themselves that help to enrich their experiences within the group and outside of the group. During the group process, the facilitator should encourage members to provide feedback to one another on an on-going basis.

The JOHARI Window (Luft, 1984) is widely used as a framework for helping group members understand the value and importance of giving and receiving feedback. It illustrates how giving and receiving feedback influences one's self-awareness and personal-social growth. The more one gives feedback and shares one's ideas and opinions, the more open and transparent one becomes to others. Conversely, the more one encourages and receives feedback from others, the more aware one becomes of how he or she is perceived and received by others.

Each person's JOHARI window has the four panes represented by four boxes where the vertical and horizontal axes intersect. The vertical axis is labeled "how I see myself, the horizontal axis is labeled "how others see me." Another way to view this is to see the vertical axis or two column boxes as representing the self; and the horizontal axis or two row boxes as representing the group. Pane one contains "things that I know about myself and things that others also know about me. This is called the "arena or open area." This is where work on the self takes place and where growth is most likely to occur. Pane two contains "things that I do not know about myself but that others know about me. This is called the "blind spot" In this pane there are important things about me that may influence or affect my interactions and relationships with others that I am not aware of but that others see and take note of during interpersonal interactions. Unless I become aware of these things my social interactions could be unproductive and perhaps even harmful to me and to others. The way I reduce this blind spot is to invite and receive more feedback from others. Pane three contains things that I know about myself but that others do not know about me. This pane is called the "façade" or "hidden area." This is the self that I present to others that may be incomplete, misleading, disingenuous and perhaps strategic. The more information that resides in this pane the less likely I am to receive the full benefit of the group's interaction because I hold back or present a self that is not sufficiently open. The way I reduce this pane and increase the group's benefit is to share more and give more feedback to others. Pane four contains information that I do not know about myself and that others do not know about me. It is labeled: the "subconscious" or "unknown." The information in Pane four may include the unhealthy over-use of defense mechanisms, repressed memories, subconscious need and desires and unknown and unexpressed motivations. It may also contain unknown potentialities and powers that become evident to the individual and the group and the giving and receiving of feedback intensifies. To experience full psycho-social and psycho-emotional growth it is important to reduce this pane and become more conscious and aware of one's thoughts, feelings, motivations, desires and needs. Reducing this pane may involve group therapy and group psychotherapy.

The size and shape of each of the four panes in the JOHARI window change as group members give and receive feedback from one another. There are four identified types of JOHARI windows based on the balance between how much and individual gives feedback and how much he or she receives feedback. The first type of window is called the "Ideal Window." This type of window represents good balance between giving and receiving feedback. In this window the arena or open area is the largest window pane and excellent work can take place as the individual experiences maximum benefit from and growth in the group. The ideal window is what individuals in groups should strive to achieve. The next type of window is called the "interviewer" window because the individual receives a great deal of information and feedback from others but shares very little and gives very little feedback. In this window the blind spot may be smaller because the individual gets much feedback but the arena is also very constricted and the façade or hidden area is large because the individual shares very little. The next type of window is called the "bull in a china shop" because the individual shares a great deal of information and gives much feedback to others but invites and receives very little feedback. In this window the blind spot is very large because the individual gets very little feedback and the arena is very constricted. The façade or hidden area may be relatively small because the individual may share and give feedback to others. The next type of window is called the "Turtle" because the individual does not share a great deal of information or gives much feedback to others and does not invite and receives very little feedback. In this window the blind subconscious or unknown is very large because the individual gets very little feedback and the arena is very constricted as are the other areas.

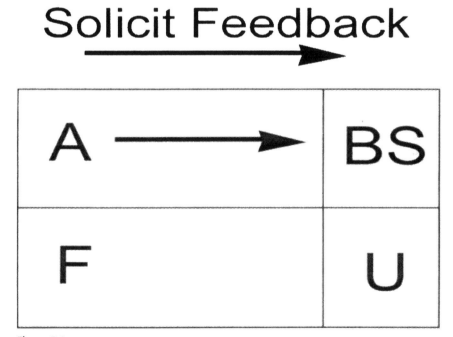

Figure 5.1.

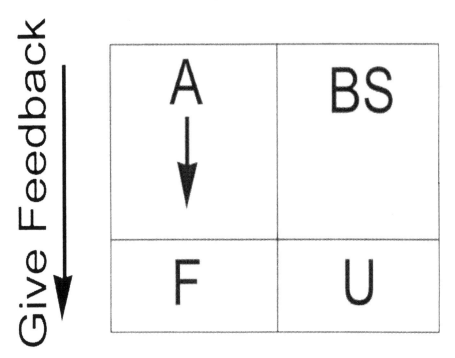

Figure 5.2.

Feedback is most effective when it is given in ways that help the recipient to process it, understand it and be able to use it. The following points about how to give feedback should be kept in mind. Feedback should be:

• focused on what a person does or says in a given situation and not on inferred motivations,
• specific and concrete, addressing the when, where and how of the behavior or statement about which feedback is given,

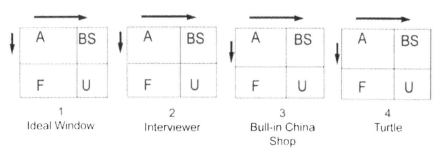

Figure 5.3.

- given as soon as possible after the target behavior or statement,
- informative about the impact of the target behavior or statement on the giver of the feedback, and
- offered in a descriptive and non-judgmental way.

CATHARSIS

Catharsis is the venting or expressing of feelings that an individual has been holding on to over a period of time. It usually occurs in therapeutic groups. The group process, including the giving and receiving of feedback in groups as discussed above, allows catharsis to occur. When catharsis occurs, the group member who has the cathartic experience purges him or herself of debilitating and regressive emotions that may hold that individual back from fully realizing his or her achievement and success potential and that limit that individual's happiness. The release of repressed feelings through catharsis allows individual healing to occur.

TRANSFERENCE AND PARATAXIC DISTORTION

In some instances, a group member may transfer or displace feelings held for someone outside of the group to the leader of the group. This is referred to as *transference*. Transference can be a healing experience for a group member and it may be beneficial to have that cathartic experience in the safety of the group. For example, a group member who is angry with his or her boss at work and who comes to the group with those feelings may direct that anger at the group leader who reminds him or her of the despised boss. When the transfer or displacement of feelings is directed at another member of the group as opposed to the leader of the group, this is known as *parataxic distortion*. The anger may be expressed verbally or non-verbally. The expression of the anger directed at the group leader or at another member in the group during the group process relieves the internal psychological pressure and emotional discomfort that the member feels.

COUNTER TRANSFERENCE

Counter transference is said to occur when a practitioner, such as a counselor or therapist, unconsciously projects or transfers unresolved feelings to a client. In a group context, the leader or facilitator of the group process may respond to a group member's expression of anger directed at him or her by becoming enraged. The group leader may castigate that member because the member reminds the group leader of his or her own sibling, with whom he or she may have had a volatile relationship. This reaction on the part of the group leader may disrupt the transference experience for the group member and compromise the therapeutic value of the interaction.

RE-ENACTMENT

The therapeutic group process sometimes allows an individual group member to re-enact or replay family dynamics which may have had significant impact on the individual's social and emotional development and condition. When family dynamics are replayed or re-enacted in the group, some group members may be the object of *parataxic distortion* and the group leader the object of *transference*. Family *re-enactment* can be a healing and growing process for the group member. Through the experience, the group member may make use of the safety of the group to address repressed emotions deeply rooted in past family experiences.

Chapter Six

Processing and Reflecting Through Journaling

with Elisa Palmieri

During the group process, reflecting on and processing group activities and experiences helps group members internalize the full cognitive and emotional impact of the group experience. The group is encouraged to process the *process*, that is, *how* the group goes about doing what it does. The group is also encouraged to process the *content,* that is, *what* topics, issues, ideas, thoughts and feelings are talked about and addressed.

JOURNALING

Journaling is an effective way for members to reflect and process group experiences. Journaling is not just a running account of what happened during a group session and which group members did and said what. It is more of a critical review of the group process and the impact of the process on the group member who is doing the journaling. It speaks to the specific events that occurred during a group session and to the significance, meaningfulness, importance, and value of those events to that member's group experience. There are six ingredients that are essential to a good journal in which a group member reflects on a group session. These are that the journal contains:

- a description and analysis of the group process including member roles and interpersonal dynamics among group members,
- an analysis of content shared during the group process,
- the group member's contribution to the group's process and to the group's content,
- the ways in which the group member who is journaling was affected by the group process and the content shared during the group process,

- an assessment of the group's progress, and
- the group member's hopes, desires and expectations for the group and for him or herself in future sessions.

Journaling is an important and essential element and evaluation criterion in a group dynamics course that the author of this book teaches over four days for nine hours each day. The major purpose of the course is to provide students with a basic and working knowledge and understanding of groups and to explore the dynamics which underlie and motivate the behavior of individuals in groups. The course involves a didactic-experiential approach to the study of individual behavior and interpersonal dynamics in groups. The experience involves students, who are the group members, as participant observers in the various aspects of group development. Students' knowledge and understanding of groups are enhanced by helping them to explore, examine and experience the principles and dynamics of group interaction through free, open and honest interpersonal interaction. The group process encourages and supports individual self-examination and self-disclosure. In the course, the journaling requirement reads as follows:

A major goal of this class is to enhance students' self-awareness and interpersonal skills, especially in a group context. To enable each student and the professor to gauge the progress that is being made in achieving this goal, each student is being required to complete and submit one journal per class/group session, detailing changes and growth in his/her self-awareness, knowledge and experiences in groups and interpersonal communication and group leadership skills. Each journal submission will include specific examples, such as anecdotes of actual experiences to support claims.

An outstanding student in this course was Elisa Palmieri, a graduate student majoring in school psychology. Elisa's journals, edited to maintain the confidentiality of group/class members, are included in this chapter. In her journals, Elisa tracked the changing dynamics in the group as the group progressed through the five stages of Wheelan's integrative model of group development. In her journal, Elisa addressed the six ingredients that are basic to a good journal mentioned above.

Journal 1: Elisa's Reflections on the First Group Session

It has taken me some time to formulate my thoughts and discuss the process and content of my experience as a member of our group today. I am taken aback by the speed at which relationships and roles within the group began to emerge and by the continual evolution of the group. Both sudden shifts prompted by disclosure and more subtle changes facilitated by small group activities moved the group through stage one of group development. As I reflect on the way I approached the initial icebreaker activity, engaging first with people I felt comfortable with and later branching out to people I did not know, I realized that, in large groups, I use the people that I am close to almost as a secure base from which to expand. I found this parallel to attachment in early childhood interesting because I always considered myself an extraverted person across contexts. When Student A summarized the strategies that different group members used to approach the task, I realized that I use perceived social supports to engage with others. Had I not known anyone in class, I am not certain that I would have been as outgoing. Moreover, these initial conversations were truly superficial because I had already made connections with the members of my cohort and knew much of the information that the questions covered and was not comfortable sharing deeper information with the members of the group who I had never met.

As Professor Haynes guided the group through processing the icebreaker activity, he directed group members into fulfilling the functions of specific roles. For example, he asked the group to summarize and provide feedback which allowed people to demonstrate the orienter role and encourager role, respectively. This subtly moved the group to a deeper level of communication. When he asked Student B to elaborate on the question about her siblings and she shared the tragic loss of her mother, the group changed dramatically. Disclosing the circumstances of her mother's death and its impact on her relationship with her sister demonstrated trust in the group members and touched each person. The group members provided encouragement and support to Student B that I believed stemmed from empathy. My reaction to Student B's disclosure was one of the utmost admiration of her strength and her ability to discuss the tragedy so eloquently, to show the impact it has had on her and they way it shaped her life without focusing on the negative aspects. While I can relate to the devastation that losing a mother at a young age has on a person, it is hard for me to imagine what it would be like to be 14 and have my father remarry six months later. When Professor Haynes asked if anyone else had lost a parent, I found my strength to speak in the courage shown my Student B. I felt that through the experience of losing a mother, a link was made, a shared experience that is so significant and pervasively impacting, yet relatively uncommon. I did not realize that I would become so emotional in discussing the loss of my mother because I have talked about it on other occasions and remained composed. However, in speaking I realized that preparing to move and going through my mother's belongings had forced me to re-experience the loss and made it difficult to discuss. I was truly touched by the feedback I received as group members were supportive, empathetic, offered advice, and made connections with what I had said. I feel that this exchange, so early in the day, set the stage for free disclosure and established a foundation of trust within the group.

When we participated in the small group "Many Circles" exercise I felt that it allowed people to form relationships with members from their small group. We were able to share information about each other and how the groups that we belong to have a dramatic influence on our lives. Also, it was interesting to see the various ways in which other members of the larger group conceptualized the task and how they went about filling in the circles. For example, Student C used school and work as the center circle because they have the most direct influence on her actions, while others and I used family as the center circle because of its influence over time. The process of filling in the circles and discussing the influence of each group elucidated how the groups that I belong to have both shaped and continually inform my identity and my self-concept. It was difficult at times to differentiate between group values and norms and my core set of beliefs and I was able to see how my personality was different across group contexts. Moreover, I became aware of how my identity and the way I see myself is through the lens of my interactions and relationships with other people. I always seek to know more about others, to form new relationships, to learn about people who have had different experiences than mine because I can take and give something beneficial from each encounter. This may reflect the emphasis that my culture places on the bond between both family and community members. In discussing the groups that I placed in my circles, both in the small group and with the larger group, I was able to see how the roles I played in those groups were carrying over to how I was interacting with the group. It made me conscious of how I was talking to other members and what I was saying and prompted me to shift focus from adding my own thoughts and experiences to another person's comments, but to asking clarification questions to understand the other people better.

The information that Student D shared about her experiences being homeschooled, the impact that it had on her peer relationships and views of friendship and family, and her family dynamics was incredibly valuable for me. Her experiences were so different from mine and from most people I have encountered and the candidness with which she explained how she felt about her family not supporting her desire to play professional tennis and the way that homeschooling has effected how she relates to people now, gave me insight into who she was. I felt that I knew and was able to understand an important element of who Student D is and how her past experiences have informed her future. Moreover, it was interesting that both Student D and Student O were homeschooled and their experiences were so different. Her disclosure marked another shift in the development of the group. With the guidance of Professor Haynes, exchanges within the larger group began to be conversations between members rather than someone using the third person or directing statements to the group at large or the facilitator.

I still feel that our group is in stage one, dependency and inclusion because members are still tentative in their communication, conflict has not emerged and conformity is high. The structure and organization within the group is still unclear and members do not yet have clear roles. Additionally, we often receive feedback on our behaviors which contributes to self-awareness, but it is not often direct and constructive. I am anxious to see how feedback from group members will inform my self-awareness.

Journal 2: Elisa's Reflections on the Second Group Session

It is incredibly difficult to synthesize the experiences of group today into a reflection. While a worthwhile experience that I have gained so much from, today was truly emotionally draining. Disclosing my feelings, thoughts and reactions as well as listening to and responding to others was enjoyable but tiring. It takes a lot of effort to engage in those activities for hours on end. Moreover, I had no idea the directions that sharing our reflections would take the group. I feel that we have evolved an immense amount in today's class. It seems as though we moved through stage two and into stage three as conflicts in values or beliefs arose, but the climate of safety, respect and encourage-ment allowed members to express differences. Subgroups also were formed as different individuals within the group formed connections based on similar experiences, personality traits and beliefs. Throughout the sharing of journals and the activities that followed, trust and cohesion were firmly established. Also, as stage three states, the group leader became more consultative than directive as Professor Haynes stepped out of the group, letting interactions play out. The growth and development of the group through the stages was facilitated by the sharing of journals and the interactions that resulted.

Coming into today's class I was anxious to receive feedback and I began taking notes about what other people said about the experience of being in a group and about my role. Student E stated that I filled the role of contributor and facilitator. I thought that this was interesting because it was very difficult for me to break free of the role of a student, who contributes information re-lated to counseling theory or practice and to allow myself to be a member of a group who was focused on the interactions. I am very comfortable with filling the role of a student while at school and I had to remind myself that while this was a class, I was a participant and member, not just a classmate. I thought that Student F's reflections were interesting because he drew comparisons between his wife, who is a school psychologist, and me and the members of my cohort. He also grounded his experiences in their application to his job, which I thought was important. At times I forgot to keep in mind, that I am learning skills and activities that I can use in my future profession. I tried to keep that in mind for the rest of the day.

Student G shared his journal and discussed how he felt that he struggled with breaking through his role of someone who makes people laugh and protects others and wanted to be able to share more. This resonated with me because in my family, my jobs, my circles of friends, I feel that I am someone who tries to make everyone else happy. I try to be everything for everyone in each group that I am a part of. I will always drop everything to help someone and I will always take on whatever responsibilities are offered to me. It made me think about whether or not this was healthy and if I needed to take more time for myself. It seems like Student G uses humor and his good nature to guard against having to share too much of himself and I realized that I do the same. It was interesting that later in the group Student G was able to share about his relationship with his grandfather and the support that he provides to his friends. He expressed that behind the jovial and funny person that livened the group, it was draining and I was able to see, how much work it is and how difficult it is to be that support for others. I did not realize the toll it takes on a person, the toll it takes on me. Student C also talked about how she is a supporter for other people and that is probably why she chose counseling. Her comments made me think about how important it is to break out of the roles that you play in life and experience other roles.

Student H discussed how it was difficult to give feedback to one person within the group which I absolutely agreed with. Group interactions in this kind of setting are alien to me and it was hard to learn how to be authentic, genuine and responsive to something someone says in a group setting. I have been making my utmost effort to compensate for sounding formal and trying to establish connections. I have tried to direct my comments towards specific individuals, creating dyads within the group and inviting others into those conversations. Student H also stated that at times she agreed with something someone said but did not tell them. I thought about this and tried to incorporate that into the rest of the day. I tried to comment on the meaningfulness of each person's contributions. I want everyone's comments to be acknowledged and supported so I have tried to express the value I saw in what people were contributing. Previously, I was thinking how interesting connections that people were making or how useful contributing a new perspective was, now I am tried to tell people that. However, I am not sure if I am talking too much and overshadowing other people in the group. Being a part of this type of a group, is a work in progress for me.

When Student A talked about how she was disinclined to share the loss of her best friend with the group after Student B and I talked about losing our mothers, I felt incredibly saddened. As Student B mentioned, she did not share because she wanted sympathy, she shared because she felt safe and she wanted to convey something about herself and in doing so set the stage for future disclosure. I have often encountered other individuals who are uncomfortable talking about losses they have experienced with me or remark that their loss was not as bad as mine. While I appreciate that they understand the devastation that losing my mother had on me, it makes me feel sad that they delegitimize their feelings regarding their losses. Everyone has and will experience losses and the significance of those losses depends on the situation. Loss has a pervasive impact on a person, and I do not believe it is fair to anyone to compare losses objectively when the experience is truly subjective. Everyone is entitled to grieve their losses and everyone can understand on some level how it would be to loss a parent, a friend, a spouse, a child or any important person in your life. I thought back to a conversation I had with Professor Y concerning issues around diversity. She asked me to consider a person who goes to counseling for sexual abuse; if that person's therapist has also experienced sexual abuse their understanding is on a deeper level and there may be a certain connection made. However, a therapist can still be effective and help that person if they have not had that experience. Similarly a doctor can still help someone who has pneumonia, even if they have never had it. She used these examples to illustrate how a person of the majority population can still advocate against and have some understanding of the injustice faced by marginalized populations.

The support group that grew out of the discussion of Student A's journal was extremely cathartic and therapeutic, but incredibly draining. It was so helpful for me to hear the experiences of the other people in that inner circle and to talk about them. Student B, who has been a support for me since the beginning, offered me advice on letting my feelings out sometimes and she did so in the most respectful and encouraging way. It was very meaningful for me. Another aspect of the support group that I found very meaningful was that Student I had the courage to come forward, with some gentle prodding by myself and Student J. Student I is one of my close friends and I knew about the murders of her sister-in-law and niece. She is someone who is more reserved and quiet at times, a listener who is incredibly empathic and kind. She will make a wonderful counselor. I have nothing but respect and admiration for the strength it took for her to come forward and speak about that experience. I felt a connection with each person in that support group, a bond that was very deep. Despite the fact that we had experienced very different kinds of losses, the grieving process was still similar, and the emotions we felt were still the same. The discussion that followed the support group was no less meaningful. I felt that it encouraged everyone to open up about losses that they have experienced, when they may not otherwise have shared. In that we all connected. I was incredibly taken aback by the display of emotion by Student K. She is such a strong person, perhaps because that is the role she plays in her family. I know that it took a lot for her to open up and I appreciated it so much. I felt that she was able to let the group in and I was so glad to be a part of that because I do respect her so much.

The connections between different members of the group surfaced through the remainder of the discussion of journals. Student C, Student G, Student F and Student L connected through their experiences supporting other people. Student C, Student L and Student I connected through their introverted nature and the process of opening up and sharing personal information. Student D and Student H connected over reestablishing identity when you no longer do an activity that you defined yourself by. I strongly feel that identity will be revisited throughout the lifespan. Each time someone faces a transition, or has a significant experience, their identity is re-evaluated. Not only this, but their meaning must be established anew. Student M demonstrated this as he talked about the ways in which his life and view of himself has changed so dramatically after having a son. Additionally, I thought that Student O's comments on how for a group to be effective you need many different roles, you need listeners and leaders, contributors and encouragers.

As a closing thought, what Student M said about feeling that counseling was for the weak-minded prior to seeing how it helped his brother stuck with me. I could not believe that I had forgotten that people felt that way, that there is still stigma around counseling. As someone who plans to provide counseling as a part of their profession, I only saw it as something beneficial and at times necessary. Even though we talk about stigma in class, to hear someone outside the counseling profession talk about it really made its influence clear. Moreover, it made me think about how I view counseling. I think that counseling is something that everyone can benefit from, that can make everyone a better person, not just those with psychopathology. I have yet to meet someone who does not have problems and could not benefit from being more self-aware. Whether I thought I needed to be a group or not does not detract from the fact that this group is making me a better person, professionally and personally.

Journal 3: Elisa's Reflections on the Third Group Session

I am astounded at the development of our group and how we have moved through the stages of group development. I feel that we are a cohesive group that was able to discuss issues that we had differing opinions on in a accepting and understanding manner. I feel safe within the group and I feel that it goes beyond trust to forming relationships that I hope to maintain. It seems as though we all feel comfort and safety within the group and some of the tasks involved in group interactions were once awkward have become familiar. In Wheelan's five stages of group development, a characteristic is "The group has an open communication structure in which all members participate and are heard." I feel that this statement accurately describes our group.

As we shared our journals today I noticed many more people taking notes because they wanted to remember the contributions of other group members and I feel that this was a meaningful transition. A theme in the journals was how emotionally draining, but rewarding the previous weekend was. It was a difficult process, but it was not without enjoyment. When I shared my journal, which served as a summary from last Sunday, I mentioned Student G specifically. He shared that hearing me talk about things that he said showed that I was really listening to what he was saying and he appreciated that. Student H, Student C, Student G shared that the group had prompted them to seek counseling outside of school because they became more aware of issues that they wanted to discuss and saw the benefits of counseling through our group. Many people echoed that the group served to open them to the idea of going to counseling, not just because they have a certain problem, but because it can benefit anyone. Student G stated that it meant more to hear the feedback from people that he did not know as well, because there were no motives to people sharing their views of others and the meaning they found in what others said.

I agreed with the comments that Student O and Student A made regarding the structure of the class. If the class was not as long people would not have disclosed so much and gotten so close. The long days truly pushed people to their limits and broke down walls that people had put up. Student K said they she feels she is guarded and that she allowed the group in last Sunday. One of the most important comments that I took from Student K was that you have to know yourself to truly help other peoples. Self-awareness is a requisite for the counseling profession; however, this is true of any person. You do not have to be in a counseling profession to help someone, but you do need to know your strengths and weaknesses. I feel that this group has shed light on who I am and closed the JOHARI window significantly. While, I have much room to grow, I can feel the progress that I, and others, have made in such a short time.

Another important contribution from a journal that lead to significant discussion was when Student A shared her experience in school the week prior. The group had given her the confidence and skills to reach out to a student who had lost his brother to suicide. From this comment, the group was moved to discuss the role of school counselors and ultimately school psychologists. I was able to see the limits of the profession and the ways in which we can strive for change and progress. We discussed how this class can be adapted for high school and college students and this might be a way to make school counselors and school psychologists visible in the school.

The "Getting to Know You Part Two" activity drastically differed from the first group activity. We formed subgroups and discussed issues that were listed on the sheet. In this activity I was able to find common group with each person I talked to even if our views did not align on every issue. Also, I learned a lot about Student M and his experiences in the air force. It was amazing to hear about his views on the war in Iraq as someone who witnessed the war first hand. When we brought the discussion to the group as a whole, there was an air of acceptance even if people did not agree. I felt that when Student J shared about his sister having an abortion and the hostility she experienced from others, an important point arose. For many of the issues, unless you have a personal experience, it is hard to have a firm position. When you do have a significant personal experience, it is difficult to separate that experience from the issue itself.

The activity that focused on conflict styles made me more aware of how much I accommodate and while it is required and many times beneficial in situations where I do not have legitimate power, it can be damaging to myself and my relationships. I often take on so much and spread myself so thin because I do not want others to shoulder any burdens and I want to care for the people I love. Within my family and current close group of friends, this accommodating nature is not taken advantage of, rather the people that I am closest to are often accommodating themselves. When I encounter someone who has a competing style of conflict management, I try to hold my ground but often end up backing down. After a while, I become so hurt by the relationship. I recognize that I truly want and need to be more assertive. I need to ensure that my needs are met and they deserve to be. More than anything, I realize that I have a lot of room for growth and improvement and it makes me wish we had more time in this class.

Journal 4: Elisa's Reflections on the Fourth Group Session

The last day of class was one of mixed emotions. I was excited to come in and see the whole group together, but it was truly bittersweet. It was likely that it was the last time we would all be together. However, I become closer to the individuals in my cohort and have made deep connections with other members of the group. These thoughts occupied a place in the back of my mind throughout each activity. Our group has swiftly moved through each of the stages of group development. We demonstrated the highly cohesive nature of the group, multiple subgroups including but not limited to the work groups that presented together were integrated into the larger group, and roles within the group seemed clear though not rigid. The overwhelming sense of support and recognition of the positive qualities and contributions of each of the group members overshadowed any conflict of values or opinions.

I greatly enjoyed the sociometry exercise although it was difficult to choose one person and for each category. I wanted to recognize so many different individuals for their strengths and contributions to the group and being forced to choose prevented me from commenting on each person. For example, I had a hard time choosing the person that fulfilled the therapist or counselor role. I felt a strong bond with Student B due to the shared experience of losing a mother and I feel that she gives incredibly useful advice. What's more, she does so with the utmost respect and the best interest of the other person in mind. However, Student A consistently provided support to each person in the group when they shared meaningful experiences or feelings. I also know that the members of my cohort that were in the class would be wonderful therapists and counselors. I shied away from picking one of them because I have seen firsthand their abilities to balance empathy and advice, to provide insight and reframe issues and it was too difficult to choose among them. Additionally, it was difficult to choose a best friend in the group. I chose the person who was closest to me; however, I echo the sentiments of many of the group members because I see myself having close friendships with many group members for years to come. I feel that I have made important relationships with each person in class.

It was also very interesting to see how others saw my role in the group. About half the class chose Student G as a leader, I included, and the other half chose me. I feel that Student G had many leadership qualities, particularly cuing, reflecting feelings and energizing. He has a charismatic personality that commands respect and power. It is clear that he has a lot of referent power, which draws so many people to him. It surprised me that many people chose me as a leader because I felt that I pulled back to allow others to have the opportunity to display their leadership qualities. As the class progressed many group members stepped into a leadership role. Student F directed conversations toward work application, Student A reflected others feelings and identified links between members and Student K asked questions to the group and cued others. When Student N talked about the leadership roles that he plays outside of class, I was far from surprised. Student N is firm in his beliefs, but accepting of all others. He seems to be able to take in information, synthesize and use it.

The most difficult part of this weekend was the "How Wheel" exercise. I enjoyed listening to others describe how they perceive themselves and how others perceive them. I was able to learn a great amount about each person and it was wonderful to be able to comment on what everyone shared. However, I feel very uncomfortable talking about myself. I feel that I know who I am and the people close to me know who I am, and it is something hard to explain. Talking about how I see myself make me think of both positive and negative qualities and while I can admit what I do not do well, I feel embarrassed talking about my strengths. It was a hard task to accomplish, but my classmates were tremendously supportive and I have clear direction for personal growth.

I have gained more from this group class than I can express. It is always painful to recognize your weakness, but encouraging realizing your strengths. The group was a tool for me to move toward becoming more self-aware and experiencing personal growth. I have learned so much from the shared experiences and beliefs of the members of the class. Equally important, I have taken away deep connections with sixteen other people that I will carry with me.

Activity #14: Mirror

Directions:

1. Each group member is invited to reflect on and complete the following four statements.

- In this group, I see myself as:
- In this group, I think that others see me as:
- In this group, I would like others to see me as:
- In this group, I would not like others to see me as:

2. The group then provides feedback to the member on his or her reflections.

Activity #15: Window

Directions:

1. Group members are given a copy of the JOHARI Window with each pane or quadrant in the window blank.
2. Each group member is then invited to fill in each quadrant except the unconscious window.
3. The group member shares and discusses the filled-in information in each quadrant.
4. The group provides the member with feedback.

Chapter Seven

Termination

Termination or the ending stage of a group may be viewed as a time of transition for group members. This is so because the closeness and connections experienced in group are about to change. As the group process draws to a close, group members often experience mixed emotions about the pending termination of the group. For some group members, forming meaningful relationships and bonding with other group members was a profound experience that they would miss and cherish for a very long time. Some group members address this by establishing ways to stay in touch with one another. For example during the final session of a training group the following exchanged occurred:

Group Leader,

> This being the final group session I wanted to give each of you an opportunity to reflect on what this experience has meant to you.

(about one minute silence)
Mitch,

> I suppose this is goodbye then. I never imagined that I would feel this way about leaving a group of strange people I met for the first time just a couple of weekends ago. I must say that for me, this has been a very special experience. I will miss all of you. I hope we stay in touch.

Group Leader,

> Mitch I sense deep sadness in your voice and I see that your eyes are watering a bit.

Mitch,

Yeah, you're right. This is hard for me. I have really grown close these other nine people. Goodbyes are hard for me. I know that I will see some of these folks again, but it will never be the same as it's been in this group.

Lisa,

Mitch I feel the sadness you feel about the group's ending. It's been such a wonderful learning and growing experience for me and I think for all of us. But my reaction is very mixed. I am sad yes, but I feel energized. I feel ready to take what I have learned here and go away from this group a stronger person. I cannot wait to use what I have learned here about myself in other situations out there.

Paul,

I don't know where to start with this. As you all saw in my "many circles of" activity when we discussed the groups in our lives, I belong to many groups. I needed more circles to cover all the groups that I am a part of. Yet I never really considered groups in the way we looked at groups here. So I am taking away a new appreciation for the importance of groups. But also, this group gave me a new way of looking at myself and the issues that I shared with you. I never in my wildest dreams imagined that I could express in a group such as this the anger and frustration I expressed. So for me, this experience was worth the sacrifice of my weekends. I would definitely do this again in a heartbeat. Thanks to all of you!

Ramona,

Can I say this? I really appreciate how far we have come from a simple ice-breaker on the first day to the trust that we have been able to develop in one another. You all are amazing people. Sure, I said some things to Kim when we had a disagreement, when we were in stage two as a group. I meant it then when I used the "B" word but guess what, I did not know you as well as I know you now (turning to face Kim). I took what you said as insensitive and self-centered. But guess what, I came to appreciate you for your honesty and openness about your feelings and I really look up to you as someone I can learn from. I hope that we can stay in touch after the group ends. And, maybe we can make an email list to stay in touch.

Kim (making eye contact with Ramona),

You know Ramona, I am so glad that we worked through our feelings. I like you a lot too. I definitely want to stay in touch with you.

Kim (making eye contact with the rest of the group)

> Maybe we can have a reunion sometime because this has been such a terrific experience and meeting again even in a social way as a group might be fun. I wish all of you the best. I know that I am taking away very good insights about myself that I know for sure will help me be a better person. Thanks Ramona and thanks to all of you. Good Luck guys!

As the vignette shows, group members explore ways of trying to maintain some of the camaraderie and connections that are established during the group experience. With the networking capabilities of the internet group members are more able now than years ago to stay connected and maintain valuable friendships that were formed during the group process. For others, the group experience allowed them the opportunity to access thoughts and feelings that they were not aware of before or may for some reasons decided to ignore or repress. Therefore, the group experience that provided opportunities for self-reflection and feedback from other group members in a climate of genuine support, candor, honesty and challenge might have been a life-altering experience. For some, termination may revive memories about previous experiences with loss and separation and conjure up feelings of abandonment, pain and hurt. These feelings may find expression in anger, resentment and resistance to termination. Still for others, the group experience may have fallen short of their expectations for themselves and for others in the group. Whatever the impact or lack of impact of the group experience on the group as a whole and on individual members, termination is a time for one last reflection and for thinking about what one would take away from the experience that might be valuable and useful.

The skilled group leader is able to help group members process and address the range of emotions that may surface and to take from the group what each member needs to take. One of the ways that the group leader does this is to invite group members to reflect specifically on the insights that they that they may have learned about themselves and the lessons that they may be taking away from the group experience. For example:

Group Leader,

> I wonder what new insights about your own personal growth each of you might be taking away from this group experience. I also wonder if there are specific lessons that you have learned about being in a group such as this that you are taking away that may influence how you would engage with groups in the future.

Robin,

> I can talk for another hour or more about the insights I have gained and the lessons I have learned so let me try to summarize, using the summarizing skills I have learned here (group laugh). For me the JOHARI window was such a revealing way to see myself in a way I never saw myself before. My blind spot was as large as Mars. I mean you guys helped me to see so many things that I was totally unaware of in myself from my biting on my thumb nail to using the phrase "you guys" even when I am talking to women and smiling when I am expressing a sad thought. I really need to work on those things. As far as engaging with groups in the future, I definitely feel that my new knowledge of conflict resolution styles and what my style is as well as the power bases and my power quotient or PQ will help be more effective with people. I can see myself at work doing much better and getting better results; yeah definitely.

Craig,

> Robin I can listen to you talk all day long. For me I realize that I need to work through my feelings about my Dad. I now have a clearer picture in my head about what my relationship with him can be like and not focus so much on what the relationship should be like. As far as other groups, I know that I will be a more effective member of the groups I am a part of. The thing that stood out for me as a coach was how to get my players to be more motivated and to go the extra mile. I like the idea of decision by consensus although I know it takes time. But for me in my coaching, I think it is the way to go. Not too many coaches I know would go for consensus. They would be more "autocratic" than "democratic" even though they may use voting from time to time. But about using consensus, they would say no way. I feel that it can be a tool to help my players become more engaged and work harder because at least to some extent their voices are heard in a meaningful way. I also like the six Is. I will use that too.

In addition to directly inviting and receiving comments and reflections as indicated in the vignettes above, the group leader may also use an activity such as the web activity described below to encourage group members to reflect on the meaning of termination for them.

Activity #16: The Web

An activity that allows each group member to process and reflect on his or her contributions to the group and what the group has meant for him or her is called: "the web."

Directions:

1. Group members are asked to stand in a circle.
2. The group leader provides a ball of yarn long enough to be passed around to each group member.
3. The group leader gives the ball of yarn to one group member, invites him or her to hold on to the loose end of the ball of year and to pass the other balled-up end to another group member across from him or her in the circle.
4. As he or she does so, he or she reflects on what he or she brought and gave to the group process and shares this with the other members.
5. This process is repeated until the ball of yarn is passed to each group member with each group member continuing to hold on to the yarn as he or she passes the balled-up end of the yarn to another member.
6. The result is that a web is formed. The group leader comments on the web indicating that the web represents the bonds, the connections, the shared thoughts, ideas, feelings and feedback that made the group experience what it was. Now at termination the web is about to be broken.
7. Each group member one by one is invited to reflect on and to say what he or she was taking way from the group and as he or she did so to release the end of the web that he or she was still holding. The process is repeated until each group member has released the web.
8. The group leader declares that the group is terminated.

Chapter Eight

Conflict and Power: Patterns of Influence in Groups

Many group members fear and shy away from conflict. They tend to see conflict as a negative development that may damage relationships among group members and result in hurt feelings. However, conflict is an important part of the group development process that helps to move the group forward. Often on teams, which are, for the most part, work groups, conflicts arise when decisions have to be made. There may be different ideas about what the best decisions may be or there may be unhappiness with the manner in which some members may communicate their preferences. In therapeutic groups, conflicts tend to center around personalities, perceptions, values and behaviors in the group. Regardless of the type of group, the sources of conflict within groups generally include the following:

- the group's purpose and goals are ambiguous,
  members' roles and responsibilities are undefined and unclear,
- expectations for the group are unrealistic,
- communication between the group leader and group members or among group members is unclear,
- information that is shared between the group leader and group members or among group members is incorrect or misleading,
- there are real or perceived differences in group members' needs and priorities,
- there are real or perceived differences in values, attitudes or beliefs among group members,
- members have conflicting ideas and positions on issues,
- there are gender, racial, ethnic or cultural differences among group members, and
- there is a lack of trust between the group leader and group members or among group members.

During stage two of a group's development conflict tends to occur. Wheelan (1994) called this stage the counter-dependence and fight stage, the name of the stage suggesting that group members no longer depend on the group leader as they did in stage one but are now more assertive in expressing their differences with the leader and with one another. Thus, conflicts suggest a struggle for independence from the leader and greater confidence in challenging the leader and one another. Conflict emerges in stage two as a natural step in the evolution of the group with any one or any combination of the factors identified above serving as the source. The resolution of conflict propels the group forward and raises the group's performance profile to a higher level than before the conflict occurred. Group members are likely to emerge from the conflict and the resolution collectively empowered, energized, willing to trust one another and more committed to the success of the group.

CONFLICT RESOLUTION

Group members feel differently about conflict and approach conflict differently. Thomas and Kilman (Thomas & Kilman, 1974, 2007) suggested that there are five basic conflict resolution styles or modes that people use in situations where they face conflict. The definitions and explanations of these five conflict resolution modes taken from Thomas and Kilman (1974, 2007) are discussed below.

Conflict Resolution Modes

1. Competing is assertive and uncooperative—an individual pursues his own concerns at the other person's expense. This is a power-oriented mode in which you use whatever power seems appropriate to win your own position—your ability to argue, your rank, or economic sanctions. Competing means "standing up for your rights," defending a position which you believe is correct, or simply trying to win.
2. Accommodating is unassertive and cooperative—the complete opposite of competing. When accommodating, the individual neglects his own concerns to satisfy the concerns of the other person; there is an element of self-sacrifice in this mode. Accommodating might take the form of selfless generosity or charity, obeying another person's order when you would prefer not to, or yielding to another's point of view.
3. Avoiding is unassertive and uncooperative—the person neither pursues his/her own concerns nor those of the other individual. Thus he/she does not deal with the conflict. Avoiding might take the form of diplomatically

sidestepping an issue, postponing an issue until a better time or simply withdrawing from a threatening situation.

4. Collaborating is both assertive and cooperative—the complete opposite of avoiding. Collaborating involves an attempt to work with others to find some solution that fully satisfies their concerns. It means digging into an issue to pinpoint the underlying needs and wants of the two individuals. Collaborating between two persons might take the form of exploring a disagreement to learn from each other's insights or trying to find a creative solution to an interpersonal problem.

5. Compromising: is moderate in both assertiveness and cooperativeness. The objective is to find some expedient, mutually acceptable solution that partially satisfies both parties. It falls intermediate between competing and accommodating. Compromising gives up more than competing but less than accommodating. Likewise, it addresses an issue more directly than avoiding, but does not explore it in as much depth as collaborating. In some situations, compromising might mean splitting the difference between the two positions, exchanging concessions, or seeking a quick middle-ground solution. (Thomas and Kilman, 1974, 2007)

Each of the conflict resolution styles falls somewhere along two basic dimensions: *assertiveness*, the extent to which an individual attempts to satisfy his or her own needs or priorities, and *cooperativeness,* the extent to which the individual tries to satisfy the needs or priorities of another person or persons. The assertiveness dimension is on the vertical axis and increases from bottom to top so that the higher the score in ascending order, the more assertive the individual. The cooperativeness dimension is on the horizontal axis and increases from left to right so that the higher the score from left to right, the more cooperative the individual. This is depicted in figure 8.1.

As seen in figure 8.1, the competing style is very high on the assertiveness dimension and very low on the cooperativeness dimension. The collaborating style is very high on both the assertiveness dimension and the cooperativeness dimension. The avoiding style is low on both the assertiveness and cooperativeness dimensions. The accommodating style is very low on the assertiveness dimension and very high on the cooperativeness dimension.

Conflict Mode Instrument

Thomas and Kilman (1974) developed an instrument that is called the Thomas-Kilman Conflict Mode Instrument. It is a 30 item self-administered

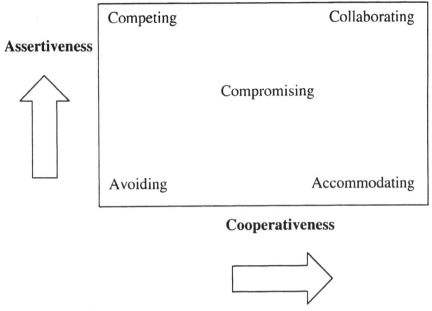

Figure 8.1.   Conflict Resolution Styles Framework.

survey that requires the respondent to select between two possible response choices for each item, choice A or choice B. When this writer uses this instrument in teaching group dynamics, the directions are modified slightly and the respondent is asked to think of situations in which he or she may have differing or conflicting points of view, ideas, positions or wishes than others. These situations may include group situations that they identified during "The Many Circles of" group activity including: family groups, work groups, friendship groups, groups at work, athletic teams, school-based teams or others. They are directed to indicate how they usually address the differences or conflicts that they have with others.

They are then directed to the 30 items on the survey and told that on the following pages are pairs of statements describing possible behavioral ways of responding. For each pair of possible responses please circle the "A" or the "B" statement that is most characteristic of your own behavior. They are also told that in many cases, neither the "A" or the "B" statement may be very typical of their behavioral response but that they should select the response that they would be more likely to use. Each conflict resolution style is assessed by 12 of the 30 items, with two of the five being assessed at the same time by any given item. The highest possible score for each conflict resolution style is 12. Below are examples of items that measure the five conflict resolution styles:

- A). I sometimes avoid taking positions that would create controversy (Avoiding)
- B). If it makes other people happy, I might let them maintain their views (Accommodating)
- A). In approaching negotiations, I try to be considerate of the other person's wishes (Accommodating)
- B). I always lean toward a direct discussion of the problem (Collaborating)
- A). I am firm in pursuing my goals (Competing)
- B). I try to find a compromise solution (Compromising).

When an individual has completed the survey, he or she then transfers his or her choices to a scoring sheet where he or she totals the score for each conflict resolution style based on the number of selected choices to the 12 questions that assessed that conflict resolution style. Following the scoring, the individual then transfers his or her total scores to a profile sheet that contains the percentile ranks for scores based on the normative data. This enables the individual to compare their conflict resolution profile with that of the normative or standardization sample. The individual can also profile their relative scores for each conflict style as depicted in figure 8.2. Table 8.1 and figure 8.3 present an example in which the choice for each item is in bold print and the total scores for each conflict resolution style are presented. Figure 8.2 indicates that the group member scores highest on the collaborating style and lowest on the avoiding style. However, when considered in relationship to the standardization sample the score for collaborating falls between the 40th and 50th percentile and the score for avoiding falls just above the 20th percentile.

As Thomas and Kilman (1974) noted:

> Each of us is capable of using all five conflict-handling modes. None of us can be characterized as having a single style of dealing with conflict. But certain people use some modes better than others and, therefore, tend to rely on those modes more heavily than others—whether because of temperament or practice.
>
> Your conflict behavior in the workplace is therefore a result of both your personal predispositions and the requirements of the situation in which you find yourself. The TKI is designed to measure this mix of conflict-handling modes.

Table 8.1.

Styles/ Item #	Competing (Forcing)	Collaborating (Problem Solving)	Compromising (Sharing)	Avoiding (Withdrawal)	Accommodating (Smoothing)
1.				A	*B*
2.		*B*	A		
3.	*A*				B
4.			A		B
5.		A		*B*	
6.	B			*A*	
7.			*B*	A	
8.	A	*B*			
9.	B			*A*	
10.	*A*		B		
11.	*A*				B
12.			*B*	A	
13.	*B*		A		
14.	*B*	A			
15.				B	*A*
16.	B				*A*
17.	A			*B*	
18.			B		A
19.		*A*		B	
20.		*A*	B		
21.		B			*A*
22.	B		*A*		
23.		A		B	
24.			*B*		A
25.	*A*				B
26.		B	*A*		
27.				A	*B*
28.	A	*B*			
29.			*A*	B	
30.		*B*			A
Total	5	7	6	4	5

Activity #17: Conflict Share

This activity involves sharing and feedback on conflict resolution style profiles among group members.

Directions:

1. Group members are invited to complete the Thomas-Kilman Conflict Resolution Mode Instrument.

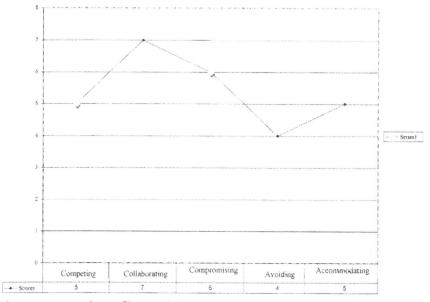

Figure 8.2.   Sample Conflict Resolution Style Profile.

2. They are asked to score and profile their scores.
3. They are invited to share their profiles in small groups of three.
4. Each group member discusses his or her profile, indicating the extent to which the profile accurately reflects their usual approach to conflict and citing at least two specific examples of when and how they used conflict resolution.

POWER

The concept of power and the notion of having power sometimes cause some people to become very nervous and they may deny a desire for power or disclaim any interest in obtaining power. Power is not necessarily a bad or negative thing to want, or to have. It is in fact a desirable way to effect positive change. *Power* may be defined as the potential or ability to influence others. Knowing the source of one's power and how one can increase one's power can be extremely beneficial to a group member in his or her interactions with other group members. The sources of power are referred to as power bases. They include in alphabetical order: *coercion, connection, expertise, information, legitimacy, reference, and reward* (Raven, 1993).

Coercive Power

When an individual is in a position to punish others if they do not do as the individual desires or instructs, the individual is considered to have coercive power. People usually act to avoid punishment. Coercive power is sometimes seen as the flip side of reward power. For example, a teacher can reward students and can also punish students based on whether or not students' do as the teacher requires. Similarly, parents can reward or punish their children based on whether or not their children obey or disobey them. In group situations an effective punishment is social disapproval. Group conformity is sometimes achieved through the coercive power that the group leader and the group as a whole are able to wield over group members.

Connection Power

Knowing people in positions of influence sometimes works to an individual's advantage and may give an individual connection power when interacting with others in a group. Others in the group may see some benefit in associating with the individual who has connection power because that individual's associations with influential persons may open doors of opportunity for others in the group. Connection power is not just limited to knowing people in high places. The ability to network with others who are in positions to support what one does or what one needs can also lead to connection power. Others may be influenced by someone who is well connected through social or professional networks.

Expert Power

A group member with expert power is someone who has the specialized knowledge, information, skill and experience that the group needs. On a Planning and Placement Team (PPT), in a school, for example, the specialists such as the school psychologist, school counselor, school social worker, speech therapist, special education teacher and licensed clinical counselor all bring expert knowledge and skills to the team and influence the team's decisions in different but equally important ways. The school psychologist for example, in addition to counseling skills, brings the specialized skills and knowledge on psycho-educational and personality testing and can share a perspective about a child's cognitive functioning and behavior that no other team member can bring. Similarly, each of the other team members, because of their expertise, can bring a specialized perspective that the other team members cannot bring. Expertise gives the individual a significant amount

of power in the context of organized groups, and outside the context of organized groups, in relationships with others.

Information Power

An individual is said to have information power when he or she has information which can influence the behavior of others. This information is
not specialized information as with "expert power" but general information that may help to inform or shape a discussion or decision. In many
group situations, the individual who is the most informed and or the most
experienced has a great deal of influence over how group members think
about issues and act on decisions that have to be made. Certainly in work
groups in which factual information helps to inform and shape decisions,
the person with the most relevant knowledge has a great deal of influence.

Legitimate Power

In many group situations, power is acquired or bestowed on an individual by
virtue of that individual's position or role in the group. The individual who
occupies a leadership position may make decisions and establish rules that determine how other people can act and under what conditions. Thus, members in
the group may respect the office that the leader holds and follow the leader's di-
rectives because that person is the leader. For example, in stage one of a group's
development the assigned leader is expected to offer guidance and direction
mostly because that person has the title of leader or facilitator. But notice what
happens in stage two. New leadership emerges among members of the group as
legitimate power is challenged and other forms of power such as referent and
information power begin to assume more relevance and strength.

Referent Power

Referent power is power that is derived from personal attributes that other
people admire and wish to emulate. When a group member is perceived
to have admirable qualities, such as thoughtfulness, kindness, confidence,
honesty as well as the attributes that are considered to be possessed by many
group leaders (these will be considered in chapter seven), then other group
members often desire to be like that person. Therefore, they may be influenced by that person's thinking and actions in the group.

Reward Power

When an individual is in a position to provide rewards to others for acting in
approved ways, the individual is said to possess reward power. This form of

power is very commonly used, but is not often perceived as a form of power by those who use it. The teacher in a classroom has, not only legitimate, information, expert and perhaps referent power, but also has a great deal of reward power. The teacher rewards students for academic performance as well as for attitudes and behaviors displayed in the classroom. In fact, much of the basis for behavior management and functional behavior analysis is premised on the concept of reward power; modifying behavior through the deliberate and effective use of rewards. Reward power is often used in groups and on teams. One of the most effective rewards in the group context is social approval. Group conformity is often achieved through the reward power that the group leader and the group as a whole is able to extend to group members.

The shift in power bases as a group's development progresses is often at the core of the changing dynamics within groups. As noted earlier in this chapter, during stage one, the assigned leader enjoys legitimate power as group members experience dependence and a need to feel included and guided by the leader. However, as group members gain confidence, are willing to take more risk, begin to bond with one another and become more aware of their strengths, the legitimacy of the assigned leader's power is challenged. This allows new leadership, based on other power bases such as reference, information and perhaps expertise, to emerge. This shift has very important implications for the group and the accomplishment of the group's work.

The Power Bases Inventory has been used to help individuals assess their power bases, and to look at which power bases they assess to be their strongest and weakest. This assessment can help individuals determine ways to enhance their power in groups and perhaps outside of groups. The Power Bases Inventory is a self-assessment tool that is comprised of 28 items to which respondents are required to answer on a likert-type, five point scale. The items are worded so that a five is the highest score and one the lowest for each item. Each of the seven power bases is assessed by four items. Below is an example of one question each for each of the four power bases:

- I usually try to sanction or reprimand others who may not follow the rules or norms (Coercive Power).
- I know people in the right places who can help others to get what they need or want (Connection Power).
- I have the ability to do a better job than others at different tasks (Expert Power).
- I provide others with information which helps them to make decisions (Information Power).
- I have a position of authority in a group or groups and use that position to influence the behavior of others (Legitimate Power).
- I have the kind of characteristics that others would like to have (Referent Power).

- I like to acknowledge and compliment others when they perform well (Reward Power). (Raven, 1993)

The total score for each power base is the sum of the scores for each of the four items that assess that power base. Therefore, the total possible score for a power base is 4 x 5=20. After completing the power base inventory each individual sums up the scores for each power base and transfers the information to a power base profile sheet. Presented in table 8.2 is an example in which the score for each item and the total score for each power base are presented in bold print. The x's represent the items that were used to assess the power bases.

Table 8.2 indicates that the group member is strongest in referent power with a score of 15 out of a possible 20. This is an individual who, based on her self-assessment, seems to influence others by virtue of her personal attributes that others admire and would like to emulate. It would be instructive to her and to the group to explore with her what those attributes are and under what conditions she demonstrates those attributes. Doing so may help her become more aware of this important source of power and perhaps learn how to maximize it. Her lowest source of power is coercive power. Exploring whether this is due to not being in a position to punish or not choosing to use punishment even if in a position to do so may elucidate more of her disposition. Her legitimate, connection and reward power bases are within one point of one another at the lower end of the spectrum. It may be that she should explore ways to increase these power bases to raise even more her overall power in groups. In exploring ways to increase these power bases, she may need to become aware of the factors that may be limiting her in these areas and work to confront, address and remove these limitations. An individual may enjoy significant personal and social benefits from having more power and may also be able to help more people.

Just as one can measure and increase one's Intelligence Quotient or IQ, or one's Emotional Quotient or EQ, one can also measure and increase what this author chooses to call one's Power Quotient or PQ. When individuals increase their power bases, they are in fact increasing PQ. The PQ is calculated by expressing a person's total score on the seven power bases combined as a fraction of the total possible score on all seven power bases combined and multiplying by 100. In the example above, the group member has overall total score on all power bases combined of 57. The total possible score on all of the power bases combined is 140 (7x20). The group member's power quotient or PQ is 57/140 x 100 = 40.7 on a 100 point scale. As one considers the concept of PQ, it is important to keep in mind that no value judgment is being attached to any of the power bases. Therefore, a high score on coercive power is considered in the same way as a high score on any of the other power bases.

Table 8.2.

Total Scores/Power Bases	1	2	3	4	5	6	7	8	9	10	11	12	13	14	15	16	17	18	19	20
Coercive Power			x																	
Connection Power						x														
Expert Power										x										
Information Power											x									
Legitimate Power					x															
Referent Power															x					
Reward Power							x													

There are different ways in which individuals may increase their PQ by enhancing their power bases, particularly those that they think may be of particular benefit to them and to others in various social situations. Presented below are some suggestions for increasing power bases:

- Identify rewards that one may possess and that others may need or want. Withdraw or withhold these rewards to influence others to act in ways that are consistent with one's expectations. This can enhance one's coercive power.
- Build networks and establish connections with people especially those who are in positions of influence. This can be established by attending conferences, joining professional associations and volunteering on projects. This can enhance one's connection power.
- Find an area of interest and of need and develop specialized knowledge and skill in that area. Become an expert. This can enhance one's expert power.
- Read more generally about current affairs and new developments in one's environment to increase one's knowledge and awareness. This can enhance one's information power.
- Increase one's eligibility for and seek promotions to positions of leadership. This can enhance one's legitimate power.
- Improve one's image by being the kind of person whom others admire. This can occur through self-reflection and self-understanding. As seen in the JOHARI window, openness to receiving feedback from others can help to reduce blind spots in one's self-perception and lead to personal growth. This can enhance referent power.
- Identify rewards that one may possess and that others may need or want. Provide these rewards to influence others to act in ways that are consistent with one's expectations. This can enhance one's reward power.

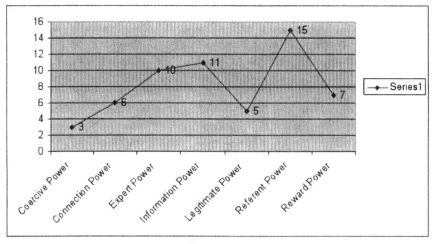

Figure 8.3. Sample Power Bases Profile.

Activity #18: Power Share

This activity involves the sharing and feedback on the power bases profiles among group members

Directions:

1. Group members are invited to complete the Power Bases Inventory.
2. They are invited to score and profile their scores.
3. They are asked to share their profiles in small groups of three.
4. Each group member discusses his or her profile, indicating the extent to which the profile accurately reflects their use of power citing at least two specific examples of when and how they used power.
5. Each group member discusses which power base he or she would like to increase and how he or she may go about doing so.

PATTERNS OF INFLUENCE IN GROUPS

The patterns of influence are important aspects of the dynamics in groups. These patterns can be tracked and can lead to an appreciation and understanding of the roles that group members play, the sources of conflict and power among group members and the leadership that emerges during the group process. In groups, different members influence group members in different ways and members identify others as influencing them in a variety of ways. One way to chart the patterns of influence in groups is through the use of sociometric techniques in which members are asked to nominate other members for identified roles in the group. The nominations are collected and then graphed in some way to show which members nominated another for the specific roles. These nominations are tallied to see which members obtained the most nominations for a given role. Examining the nominations for patterns of influence in a group is called *sociometry* and the graphic designs themselves are called *sociograms*. Sociometry and sociograms can help in knowing how best to engage a group with respect to an identified task. Individuals who receive the highest numbers of nominations may be the members in the group to turn to for help in mobilizing the group to act in certain ways. This would depend on the role for which group members have been nominated.

Below is an activity that required students in a group dynamics class to read a summary profile of group members in a group and to examine the nominations made among group members for two specifically identified roles within the group: Group Leader and Counselor/Psychologist.

Activity Sociometric #19: Influences

In a sensitivity training group (T-Group), the group members were: Bob (27, science teacher); Steve (20, student); Junie (33, business executive), Tim (40, sales representative). Tara (25, social worker); Student C (26, school psychology graduate student); Donald (59, school counselor); Sandra (30, physical education teacher); Leah (45, attorney); Larry (24, school psychologist).

The group was asked to identify one person from the group they would most likely select (A) to be their Group Leader (B) to be their Counselor/ Psychologist. The following patterns emerged:

Pattern A: Group Leader

Bob selected Tim who selected Tara who selected Donald. Tim selected Leah. Larry selected Sandra. Student C and Junie selected each other. Steve selected Tim. Donald and Leah selected Bob. Sandra selected Donald.

Pattern B: (Counselor/Psychologist)

Bob selected Steve who selected Junie. Tim and Junie both selected each other. Tara and Larry selected Junie. Student C and Donald selected each other. Sandra selected Tara. Leah selected Sandra.

Directions:

Draw the sociogram for each selection pattern, A and B, above. Give your interpretation of each sociogram pointing out any significant characteristics of the patterns, for example gender, age professional issues and other issues.

In conducting sociometric analyses, it is useful to first prepare a sociogram or graphic representation of the nomination patterns that are described in the group profile. The sociogram helps to visually inspect the patterns and enhances one's ability to conduct a more informed and careful analysis. The analysis may then focus on critical attributes of the members who are chosen for specific roles and on the attributes of group members who choose them. Presented in figures 8.4 and 8.5 are the sociograms and the sociometric analyses provided by Elisa Palmieri, one of the students in a group dynamics class taught by the author.

Pattern A: Group Leader

(* Because Tim is used twice, selecting both Tara and Leah, I only recorded that Tim selected Tara.)

Bob selected Tim who selected Tara who selected Donald. Tim selected Leah. Larry selected Sandra. Sarah and Junie selected each other. Steve selected Tim. Donald and Leah selected Bob. Sandra selected Donald. (* Because Tim is used twice, selecting both Tara and Leah, I only recorded that Tim selected Tara.)

Analysis:

Based on this sociometric diagram, it is difficult to identify one or two group members who fulfilled the role of group leader. This may be due to the fact that each of the individuals that were chosen by other group members had different types of leadership qualities. One of the trends that I was able to identify is that many members chose someone older as the group leader. Bob chose Tim, 13 years his senior; Tara chose Donald, 34 years her senior; Larry chose Sandra, six years his senior; Sarah chose Junie, seven years her senior; and Steve chose Tim, 20 years his senior. No one chose Steve, who at 20 years old was the youngest member of the group. In addition, it was more often the case that male group members chose another male as the group leader and female group members chose another female as the group leader.

It is interesting to note that the school psychologist, Larry and the school psychologist graduate student, Sarah, did not choose each other. In fact, it was rare that those in related professions chose each other. This relationship was only seen in the a social worker Tara's choice of the school counselor, Donald, the school psychologist Larry's choice of Sandra, a physical education teacher and, the school counselor Donald's choice of Bob, a science teacher. It may be that working in an educational setting with teachers, counselors and school psychologists, habituates individuals to the types of leadership qualities required for those professions. Thus, it may be easier to recognize a leader in a dissimilar profession that necessitates different skills. In turn, this may be the cause for the many members chosen as group leader.

Two group members were chosen by multiple people in the group. Tim, a 40 year old sales representative, was chosen by Bob, a 27 year old science teacher, and Steve, a 20 year old student. In addition to the fact that he is older than Steve and Bob, Tim may have been chosen because of the high interpersonal skills associated with his profession. To be successful in sales, it is necessary to be able to connect with others and to be enthusiastic in interactions. These qualities reflect two skills of an effective leader, linking and energizing, respectively. Moreover, it is possible that Tim had a charismatic personality that led to professional success and thus had high referent power. Bob was also chosen by two members, Donald, a 59 year old school psychologist and Leah, a 45 year old attorney. As a teacher, one occupies a leadership role. Bob is required to be the head of a classroom and as such he organizes summarizes and interprets material in order for his student to achieve mastery. An effective teacher truly must be a strong leader. These qualities may have lead to him being chosen by both Leah and Donald, even though they are older and may be seen as having higher status occupations. (Elisa Palmieri, April, 2010)

Pattern B: (Counselor/Psychologist)

Bob selected Steve who selected Junie. Tim and Junie both selected each other. Tara and Larry selected Junie. Sarah and Donald selected each other. Sandra selected Tara. Leah selected Sandra. This pattern is presented in figure 8.4

Analysis:

This sociometric diagram yields a clearer idea of who fulfilled the role of a counselor or psychologist within the group. Junie was chosen by Steve, Tim, Tara, and Larry. Three of these members were of the opposite gender and Steve, Tara and Larry are all younger than Junie. Overall, women were more likely to be chosen for this role as Sarah, Tara and Sandra were also chosen by group members. This may reflect the socialization of women to be more nurturing, supportive and willing to discuss emotion, which are qualities that may associated with counseling. It appears that Junie may have these qualities and a high degree of empathy, which is necessary in counselors. It is surprising that Junie, who is not employed in a helping profession, was chosen by Larry, a school psychologist and Tara a social worker. This lends credit to the assumption that she possesses qualities and skills that character-ize counselors.

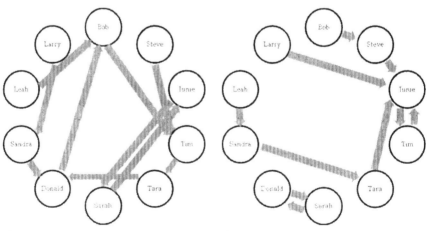

Figure 8.4.   Figure 8.5.

Three group members were chosen for the counselor roles that have corresponding professions and two of the three chose each other. Sarah and Donald chose each other. Donald, a 59 year old school counselor, has an educational background in psychology, personality characteristics that drew him to a helping field and years of experience in counseling that would make him a candidate for this role. Sarah, a 26 year old school psychology graduate student, has presumably had an undergraduate education in a psychology related field; some related work experience and is currently honing her counseling skills as a school psychologist. Perhaps, the counseling and interpersonal styles of Sarah and Donald are similar, thus forming a foundation for a successful therapeutic relationship. Tara, 25 year old social worker, was also chosen. Again, she has the educational and work experience that provide her with the skills necessary to be in a helping profession. I found it interesting that Steve was chosen for this role. He is the youngest member of the group and a student, although his level of education and area of concentration are not listed. Perhaps he is a senior majoring in psychology, or perhaps he possesses extraordinary empathy and desire to support those around him. (Elisa Palmieri, April, 2010).

Chapter Nine

Group Leadership

An effective group leader combines important attributes that group members admire and perhaps wish to emulate with essential leadership skills that are fundamental to the healthy dynamic of the group. These attributes and skills give the group leader referent power, or the ability to influence and motivate group members. The leadership attributes and skills which have been shown to contribute to effective group leadership are presented below.

EFFECTIVE GROUP LEADER ATTRIBUTES

Knowledgeable

The effective group leader has adequate knowledge of the principles of group dynamics, is deeply familiar with the type of group that he or she is leading and is sufficiently grounded in the content issue or problem area on which the group is focused. This knowledge is acquired through academic preparation, including formal and informal training, and through experience.

Competent

Closely related to but distinct from being knowledgeable is the attribute of competence. A group leader may have the theoretical knowledge, but lack the required practical knowledge and skill in group leadership. Competence is more than knowing. It is the translation of relevant knowledge into effective action. An effective group leader acquires competence through academic preparation, including formal and informal training, and through experience. The more practice with group leadership skills that the group leader has, the more competent he or she is likely to become. For group leaders who are in training or who are new to the profession it is important to have close and critical supervision by an experienced group leader. It is also very helpful to observe and co-lead groups with a more experienced and knowledgeable group leader in order to become a competent group leader.

Flexible

Effective group leadership often requires that the group leader be able to adjust his or her leadership style and group facilitation approach to accommodate changes in the group process as the group develops. The flexible group leader is also able to adjust his or her approach in different group contexts, such as in facilitating different types of groups or facilitating groups in different types of organizations. For example, the approach to facilitating a psycho-educational group with middle school students in a school setting would require a completely different approach from facilitating an anger management group with adolescents in a community-based group home. Group leaders who are able to adjust their facilitation and leadership styles well enough to be effective in different contexts may be said to be "situationally adroit." It is important to caution that flexibility should not be confused with practicing a "laissez faire" style of leadership in which the leader's engagement in the form of guidance, direction and organization is lacking. The flexible leader is fully engaged in a sensitive, proactive and responsive way. Flexibility is acquired through dedicated study, practice and experience.

Empathic or Empathetic

One of the attributes that allows the effective leader to be flexible is that leader's *empathy*, which is the ability to recognize, identify, sense, understand, and respond to the needs, feelings and ideas expressed by members of the group. Empathy, as is often explained, is not the same as *sympathy* which is feeling sorrow or pity for someone. The empathic or empathetic group leader is able to allow members of the group to experience cathartic moments in therapy groups or express ideas and feelings in non-therapy groups in an atmosphere that says we hear you, we sense where you are coming from and we are willing to see where you want to go with what you feel and think.

Attentive

To be able to express empathy, the group leader must first be able to listen and observe group members well because empathy requires focused attention to both verbal and non-verbal messages that group members send. Being attentive involves actively listening by providing encouraging and supportive acknowledgements that the leader is following and is in tune with what group members are expressing. It also involves providing indications that the group leader is in tune with non-verbal cues being consciously or unconsciously transmitted by group members. The group leader who attempts to fake attentiveness is a group leader who is doomed to fail. Effective group leadership requires *mindful attention* at all times to the interactions among group members so that every opportunity for leader impact is fully embraced by the group leader. Mindful attention means being fully focused and present in the moment, present not just physically but also cognitively, psychologically and emotionally, allowing group members to sense, know and appreciate the full and total presence of the leader.

Communicative

The effective group leader is willing and able to communicate his or her thoughts, ideas, feelings, suggestions, opinions and directions clearly, unambiguously and persuasively to group members. The issue of clarity in communicating his or her message is important given the far reaching impact that the group leader can have on group members and the group process. An essential aspect of being communicative is checking in with group members to be sure that the message being sent by the leader is the message being received by the by group. If there is miscommunication the leader addresses the cause and how to remedy the discrepancy between the sent and received message. Also of importance is the leader's *assertiveness,* being forthright and supportive in providing direct and helpful feedback to group members even if such feedback may be difficult for a group member to hear.

Inspirational/Motivational

The individual who is able to inspire others is one who can often motivate people to act in ways that effectively complete tasks that lead to the accomplishment of stated goals. The inspirational and motivational group leader inspires group members' confidence, builds trust and mobilizes and energizes others to meet challenges that arise in moving toward achieving the group's goals. Being inspirational and motivational is a significant attribute when one looks at group leader's possession of referent power.

Trustworthy

The trustworthy leader is one who is *credible, honest* and *reliable.* The Leader is *credible* or believable in terms of factual information that the he or she may share and in terms of opinions and ideas that the leader may offer to the group. The leader is *honest* in expressing his or her feelings and thoughts and in giving helpful feedback to members of the group. The leader is *reliable* in following through on commitments and promises made to members of the group. Central to trustworthiness as a group leader is the sense among group members that leader is credible, honest and reliable when it comes to protecting the confidentiality of the information disclosed by group members during the group process.

Activity #20: Leadership Attribute Interview

In this activity, the group is divided into dyads. The members of the dyads interview each other about their leadership attributes using the Leadership Interview Grid below. The grid may also be used for self-reflection. On the grid the attributes discussed above are listed in the leftmost column. In the second column from left, the interviewer in the dyad writes the response to the question regarding how much of an attribute the interviewee thinks he or she possesses. The possible responses are: "None at All"; "Some"; "Much"; "Very Much." The interviewer asks the interviewee to explain his or her response. In the next column, the third column from the interviewer in the dyad writes the response to the question regarding how much of an attribute the interviewee thinks he or she would like to acquire and how. The possible responses are: "None at All"; "Some"; "Much"; "Very Much." The interviewer asks the interviewee to explain his or her response. In the last column, the interviewer writes feedback, comments and any other points of discussion that occurred during the interview. This process should take

Table 9.1.

Group Leadership Attributes	How Much of Each Attribute Do You Possess?	How Much of Each Attribute Do You Wish to Acquire and How?	Feedback, Comments and Discussion
Knowledgeable			
Competent			
Flexible			
Empathic or Empathetic			
Attentive			
Communicative			
Inspirational/ Motivational			
Trustworthy			
• Credible			
• Honest			
• Reliable			

about 20 minutes. The roles are then reversed and the process is repeated. Following the interviews, the larger group convenes and each dyad processes first the process and then processes the content of their interviews including their feedback, comments and any discussions that occurred during the interviews.

The grid can also be used as a self-administered survey instrument or as an instrument that is objectively completed by others who know and observe the group leader. When used as a survey, the instrument can be scored and a Leadership Attributes Profile based on the scores can be prepared. After carefully reading and understanding the explanation of each leadership attribute, the individual is required to indicate how much of each attribute he or she thinks that he or she possesses by placing an (X) in the relevant box after each attribute. The possible total score for each attribute is 4. For the trustworthy attribute, each of the three dimensions: credible, honest and reliable receives a separate score. The trustworthy attribute total score is the sum of these three dimensions divided by 3. The possible total score for all of the attributes combined and for the instrument as a whole is 32.

In the example presented in table 9.2 and figure 9.1, the profile indicates an individual who scores highest on the leadership attributes of being knowl-

Table 9.2.

Group Leadership Attributes	None 0	Little 1	Some 2	Much 3	Very Much 4	Score	Comments
Knowledgeable					X	4	
Competent				X		3	
Flexible					X	4	
Empathic or Empathetic			X			2	
Attentive				X		3	
Communicative		X				1	
Inspirational/ Motivational		X				1	
Trustworthy						3	
• Credible					X		
• Honest				X			
• Reliable			X				
Total Leadership Attributes Score						21	2.6 on 4 point scale. Attribute potential of .65

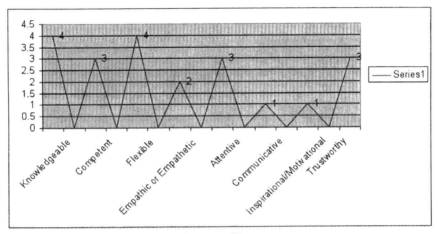

Figure 9.1. Group Leadership Attributes Profile.

edgeable and flexible and scores lowest on the attributes of being communicative and inspirational/motivational. It would seem then that this individual would need to work hard on becoming more clear and assertive in the manner in which he or she communicates with group members. This individual also needs to find ways to increase his or her ability to influence and convince others to become involved, to participate and to perform. It may be that by increasing empathy, which is also quite low, this individual may also begin to become more communicative and inspirational. The individual's leadership attributes potential which is the total attribute score on the four point scale, 2.6 divided by 4 which is .65 out of a possible 1. The goal is to reach an attribute potential score of 1.

EFFECTIVE GROUP LEADERSHIP SKILLS

Blocking

There are times during the group process that the group leader may have to interject and temporarily halt an interaction among group members to maintain the integrity of the group process and to keep group members physically, psychologically or emotionally safe. When this happens, the group leader is said to be using the leadership skill of blocking. For example, Morgan, a group member becomes irate with two other group members whom he considers to be hostile toward him. Morgan raises his voice, stands up and challenges Brennan, one of the two group members to repeat what he said before about Morgan and see what happens next.

The group leader steps in immediately and says,

> Morgan, please calm down or leave the group until you have calmed down and you are able to use the group process appropriately to address your feelings. While we want to openly express and explore our thoughts and our feelings, I would like to bring the group's attention to the norms we have agreed to as the guidelines for how we should engage with one another during the group process.

Confronting

One of the most misunderstood and under-utilized skills in group work is confronting. Confronting is directly or indirectly addressing and challenging a statement or behavior by a group member or by group members that the group leader may consider to be in need of challenge. Like the term "conflict," confronting or confrontation often conjures up images of uncontrolled anger and rage. Many individuals tend to shy away from confronting, as they do from conflict. In fact both concepts, "conflict" and "confronting" are linked in some people's minds and maybe to some extent appropriately so. Both concepts, though, are necessary and useful during the group process. Sometimes confronting may lead to conflict and that can be a healthy development for the group. For example, a group member, Rita, falls asleep several times during the group process and seems disengaged. Some group members snicker and laugh derisively as Rita nods uncontrollably, at times almost falling off of her chair. The group leader decides to confront Rita about her sleeping and to confront the group's derisive snickering, and their unwillingness to confront Rita directly. The group leader says,

> I have noticed that Rita tends to have bouts of sleepiness during the group session and sometimes seems to be falling off of her chair, yet no one says anything to Rita. In fact, some of members of this group snicker and laugh when this happens. I think that this is something we need to address as a group.

The group may not know why Rita falls asleep during the group process. She may be suffering from narcolepsy, may have trouble sleeping at night or may work all night long before coming to the group. Whatever, the reason, Rita's sleeping during the group process and the reaction of some group members seem to be disruptive to the group process and need to be confronted by the group leader. Usually, the group leader may use confronting to help the group member or members consider the undesirable or undesired effects of statements and actions and to point out the possible consequences.

Cuing

Very often in groups, group members communicate their thoughts and their feelings non-verbally. Group members' non-verbal communication usually contains messages about what they may be feeling at any moment during the group process. However, without the group leader using his or her cuing skills, these non-verbal messages may be missed and overlooked by the group. Cuing, then, is the group leader being aware of, pointing out and focusing the group's attention on non-verbal behaviors among group members. In addition, the group leader uses interpreting and questioning skills to explore the messages and meanings of the non-verbal behaviors being displayed by members. For example, Crystal, a twelve-year old girl in a psycho-educational achievement group buries her head in her hands from time to time and bounces her right foot up and down on her toes. The group leader has been observing Crystal's behavior for several minutes and then decides to focus attention on Crystal's behavior.

The group leader says:

> Crystal, I have been noticing that off and on you bury your head in your hands and bounce your feet up and down on your toes while other members of the group are sharing and talking. It seems to me that you may be feeling something or thinking about something that is making you uncomfortable. Can you share with us what you are feeling and thinking about that is making you bury your face and bounce your feet up and down.

The group leader may use cuing not just to focus the member's and the group's attention on the non-verbal behavior, but more importantly, to explore and examine the underlying message being communicated by the non-verbal behavior so that it can be addressed appropriately in the group.

Disclosing

Of all of the leadership skills discussed here, this one is probably the most debated. Disclosing is revealing information about oneself or revealing one's thoughts and feelings to others. There are some who may argue that a group leader should not disclose because doing so may take attention away from group members and place that attention on the leader. Also, disclosing may result in counter transference and may be counterproductive. There are others who argue that by disclosing the group leader shows empathy, honesty, genuineness and may in fact earn the trust of group members. The use of disclosing depends very much on the situation and the purpose for which it is being done.

For example, Melanie, a group member says

> I find that I cannot put out of my mind the picture of my mother lying there in the casket looking so cold and lifeless when I think of how beautiful and vibrant she used to be when she was alive. She loved life and never talked about dying. I think she thought like I did that she would be around forever. But just like that, in a short time she was gone. Cut down by a massive heart attack. I just don't get that. I—I feel so vulnerable now.

The group leader, in an attempt to empathize and console, Melanie says,

> I would like to invite other group members to respond. But, Melanie, first let me say that when my mother died, I felt like my world had collapsed around me. She was the light of my life. I became who I am in large part because of the mother she was to me. She was the source of my inspiration. I had to get to a place where I realized that to become paralyzed by my feelings of emptiness would be not what my mother would want. That she would want me to take the lessons she taught me about resilience, hopefulness and facing life's challenges to move on; embracing her love and the wonderful memories of times we shared, using them to become a better and more productive person.

Disclosing can be used as a form of feedback to group members as demonstrated in the example. The group leader then may use disclosing to show empathy, to motivate and to connect on an affective or cognitive level with group members.

Energizing

There are times when groups may get stuck or lose momentum. In work groups the motivation needed to complete the assigned task may decrease as team members run out of ideas and become demoralized. In therapy groups, members may become tired and emotionally and psychologically overwhelmed. When this happens, using the leadership skill of energizing the group becomes necessary. The group leader would need to get the group back on track, reignite interest in the group process and sustain momentum and verve among group members in completing the group's tasks.

For example, in a group dynamics class, the class is divided into smaller work groups to prepare projects for presentation on the final day of class. Each group has two weeks in which to prepare its project. After the first few days of e-mails, phone calls and text messaging, the group is unable to finalize a topic and begin preparing the presentation.

Leslie sends out an e-mail that says,

Look guys, we need to get our act together; the other groups are way ahead of us. I suggest we meet in person, sit down and sketch out a plan. We can meet at my place. I have outlined a plan as a start. Let's get the show on the road.

Leslie has assumed the role of energizer.

Interpreting

In some instances during the group process, members say things and behave in ways that may be suggestive of an underlying dynamic that may not be readily apparent to the group. Thus, explanation by the group leader may be required. For example, Peter, a group member turns to Joan and angrily demands an apology. Several members of the group applaud Peter and one group member, Sharon, speaks up and says, "Good for you Peter don't take any more of that B.S. from her."

The group leader interjects and says, "It is evident that Sharon and several of you feel that Peter's anger toward Joan is justified and that Joan's behavior toward Peter has been inappropriate. I wonder if we can talk about that."

The group leader may use interpreting to increase the group's awareness of the subtle dynamics and covert message that may be occurring among group members and of an individual member's subconscious behavior.

Linking

Helping group members make connections with other members of the group based on similar experiences or facts about themselves is known as linking. This skill is a very useful and important way for the group leader to help group members feel comfortable with one another and to increase feelings of affiliation, acceptance and bonding. The process of identifying with others helps to breakdown any initial barriers to communication and to open up opportunities for more informative and deeper levels of interactions. Many icebreakers are designed to encourage linking. The "Find Someone Who" icebreaking activity described earlier in this book is used to link group members and to advance the bonding process. For example, George, a group member, mentions that he has recently won an award for community service. The group leader says,

> I would like to congratulate George on his recent community service award. I am wondering if there is any other member of the group who has won an award of any kind and would like to share that with the group.

As mentioned, the group leader may use linking to give group members a sense of collective identity and to provide a common basis for trusting and for sharing at increasingly higher and deeper levels.

Questioning

Using questioning techniques to gather and clarify as much relevant information as possible from group members is an extremely important leadership skill. It is through questioning that group members are invited to share thoughts, ideas and feelings with the group that they may not otherwise share. Questions are usually classified in two kinds, *open-ended questions and close-ended questions. Open-ended questions* allow the individual to provide an expanded response to the question. *A close-ended* question limits the individual's response usually to one or two words.

For example, an open-ended question is if the group leader says to a group member,

"How do you feel about that?"

The member may say

"I feel very uncertain but hopeful."

An example of framing this question in a close-ended way is if the group leader says,

"Do you feel good about this?"

The group member may say,

"No I do not."

The open-ended question gave the group member and opportunity to say more about her feelings, that is, uncertain but hopeful. The close-ended question did not elicit much information about the member's feelings. However, close-ended questions are useful and appropriate at times, especially when the intent is to get a succinct brief response and elaboration is not necessary. The group leader may use open-ended or close-ended questions to encourage group participation and to increase interaction among group members.

Reflecting Feeling

Sometimes a group member may express feelings without describing or identifying what those feelings are. The group leader may use the group member's words to identify and describe the feelings that seem to be underlying the words expressed.

For example, group member Susan says,

> "I just don't know what to do now. I have tried everything but nothing seems to be working. I give up."

The group leader says:

> "Susan what I got from what you just said is that you are feeling frustrated and defeated. Is that how you feel?"

The group leader may use reflecting feeling to help focus the group member's attention and the group's attention on what the group member, Susan in the example, is feeling so that the feeling can be the focus of attention and can be addressed by Susan and by the group.

Reframing

The frame in which an experience is placed determines how that experience is perceived and how the individual responds to it. Reframing is taking the experience out of a frame in which it is perceived in one way, perhaps negatively, and placing it in a different or new frame that changes the way in which the experienced is perceived, perhaps positively. Reframing then involves changing the cognition and the related emotions of an experience by allowing the individual to have a different perspective of the experience.

For example, Robert was just laid off from his job as a journalist and feels that he wasted fifteen years of his life studying journalism and then working for his local newspaper.

He says,

> "I cannot believe this. I am washed up. After giving so much now I have nothing to show for it. I am done. My life is over."

The group leader decides to help Robert reframe his experience which he now sees as devastating and hopeless.

The group leader says

> "Robert, I empathize with what you are experiencing having lost your job after investing so much in your career. I wonder if this is an opportunity for you to look into starting your own independent consulting business as a free lance writer, editor and perhaps even a publisher. I remember you said during our first session that you have long dreamed about owning your own publishing business and perhaps

even becoming a known writer yourself. Well, this may be an opportunity to begin to pursue that. It may not be too late. What do you think?"

The group leader may use reframing to help group members overcome negative feelings and inertia and to encourage them to redirect attention and energy into more positive goal-directed actions. Reframing is often used in cognitive-behavioral approaches to counseling and therapy.

Rephrasing

During the group process a group member may express a thought, idea or feeling or may offer an opinion or suggestion. The group leader may rephrase what was expressed by the group member by using different words to restate what the group member said without losing or changing the essence or meaning of what was expressed.

For example, group member John says,

> "I think that Henry (another group member) does not like being put on the spot because he is afraid to be caught off guard."

The group leader says,

> "John, you seem to be saying that you think that Henry prefers not to be asked to respond without being warned because he worries about not being prepared. Is that what you are saying John?"

The group leader may use rephrasing to clarify what was said, to check with the group member to be sure that what was expressed was clearly understood or to demonstrate attentive listening.

Suggesting

In some types of groups and in some situations within a given group, the group leader's approach may be more directive than it may be otherwise; or the group leader's directiveness may be influenced by his or her theoretical orientation. The group leader may suggest some ideas or choices in addition to inviting group members to think about and to offer their own suggestions when addressing particular issues. For example, Kevin, a group member is trying to decide whether to accept a supervisory position at his job that would lead to a significant increase in salary. However, the position would at the same time require him to spend longer hours at the office and involve much more national and international travel and much more valuable time away from his family, including his one year old son.

Kevin expresses his dilemma this way.

> "This is such a great opportunity for me to advance within the company. I have looked forward to this and worked very hard for it. I also think that with the salary increase and end-of-year bonus I would be able to provide financially for my family in a way that I cannot do now. Yet, I am going to have to work twelve-hour days instead of eight-hour days and boy, I am going to have to be on an air plane almost two weeks in every month. When I think of that and how much time it is going to take way from my family and especially my one-year old son, I am not sure that it is worth it."

The group leader invites the group members to offer Kevin their feedback. Several group members offer Kevin suggestions.
The group leader then says to Kevin,

> "Kevin, this is obviously a difficult decision for you. After listening to you explain your dilemma and hearing the feedback from the group, Kevin here is what I want to suggest that you consider doing. Go to your boss and explain your dilemma. Explain your commitment to the company and your desire to advance within the company. Obviously there is something that your boss sees in you that she likes and she thinks that you have what it takes. Tell her that you would like to discuss with her a redefinition of the job that would take full advantage of your talents and commitment and allow you to be at home as often as possible to be the kind of parent to your son that you need to be. Make it a conversation and discussion. What do you think about this suggestion?"

The group leader may use suggesting to broaden the range of alternatives being considered by group members or to energize the group.

Summarizing

During the group process there tends to be different thoughts, ideas, feelings and suggestions that are presented for group members to consider and discuss. It is useful for the group to pause periodically and to reflect on the collection of material that the group has been addressing.

For example, the group has been sharing their thoughts and feelings about what it is like to be discriminated against based on a variety of factors. Jan says,

> "In this group I am the oldest. In fact, I feel really old because the rest of you are so damn young. I mean, pretty girl over there is only 20 and you Steven, you are just turning 22. I feel like I am grandma here and I can sense that sometimes you feel that I am overbearing and too controlling. I think that, although you have not come out and said so, that it is all because of my age."

Carl, bristles a little and says,

> "You know I can identify with that. As a brown skin Latino male I feel that
> people often expect me to fit into one of their stereotypes about what Latino
> males are supposed to be like and here in this group I feel the same way. You
> know I was the first person in the group today and when people came in they sat
> next to everybody else until the only seat left was the one next to me and that's
> why Bev is sitting next to me now."

Daphne speaks up. She turns to Carl and says,

> "You know Carl; you are so right on with that. When I came in there were just
> two seats left and I took this one and I just don't know why. I mean, I am not
> prejudiced or anything like that. But really, it would have been so much easier
> for me to have sat next to you than to walk all the way around to sit here. Wow!
> That is an eye opener for me."

Jadeen then opens up and says,

> "This irks the day life out of me. Why do people dislike or distrust other people
> just because of what they look like or because of who they are. I am gay and
> I get that all the time. Now that I have disclosed that I am gay I am sure that
> most, if not all, of the people in this group are going to view me differently and
> maybe treat me differently. I hate that. Why can't we just see people for whom
> they are; people just like we are?"

After a longer period of sharing and discussion the group leader says,

> "So let me summarize what we have shared and discussed so far. Some of you
> have experienced what it is like to experience prejudice and to feel rejected or
> to be treated negatively because of whom you are and what you look like. Jan,
> Carl and Jadeen shared their feelings about being treated differently or with
> prejudice because of who they are. Daphne was honest about her actions when
> she came to the group earlier this morning and seemed to subconsciously avoid
> sitting next to Carl. My sense is that most of you, if not all of you, think that
> prejudice of any kind is wrong and that the person who practices prejudice and
> discrimination is a loser. Is that a fair enough summary?"

The group leader then pauses and waits for a response. Group members nod
their approval.

The group leader then says,

> "Now where do we go with this next?"

The group leader may use summarizing to help group members reflect on and
to further consider in an even deeper level issue or issues that the group has

discussed and to give the group a sense of orientation and direction moving forward.

Supporting

The leadership skill of supporting involves the group leader offering words and actions of encouragement or reinforcement to group members and inviting other group members to do the same. There are times when group members may feel frustrated or inadequate in the group or may doubt the value of their contributions to the group process. The group leader may sense this or this may be directly expressed by a group member.

For example, Bevin feels that he is not as well prepared to participate in the sensitivity group as other group members because, unlike other group members, he is not in one of the helping professions.
He says,

> "I am not sure what I have to offer you guys because you are all familiar with the psycho babble stuff and know how to feel what other people feel. I don't."

The group leader says,

> "Is there anyone who would like to share with Bevin what you think about what he just shared about how he feels being part of this group?"

Sandra says,

> "Bevin, let me tell you this. When I first came to this group you were the first person I spoke to and I was impressed on how warm and comfortable it was to talk with you. Since then you have shown all of us what it means to listen to people, empathize with them and be an effective group member. So, I see you as being so important and valuable to this group."

The leader then turns to Bevin and asks,

> "Bevin, what do you think about the feedback Sandra just gave you? Please tell her."

Activity #21: Leadership Skills Interview

In this activity, the group is divided into dyads. The members of the dyads interview each other about their leadership skills using the Leadership Skills Interview Grid below. The grid may also be used for self-reflection. On the grid the skills discussed above are listed in the leftmost column. In the second column from left the interviewer in the dyad writes the response to the question regarding how much of a skill the interviewee thinks he or she possesses. The possible responses are: "None at All"; "Some"; "Much"; "Very Much." The interviewer asks the interviewee to explain his or her response. In the next column, the third column from the interviewer in the dyad writes the response to the question regarding how much of a skill the interviewee thinks he or she would like to acquire and how. The possible responses are: "None at All"; "Some"; "Much"; "Very Much." The interviewer asks the interviewee to explain his or her response. In the last column, fourth from left, the interviewer writes feedback, comments and any other points of discussion that occurred during the interview. This process should take about 20 minutes. The roles are then reversed and the process is repeated. Following the interviews, the larger group convenes and each dyad first processes the process and then processes the content of their interviews including their feedback, comments and any discussions that occurred during the interviews.

The grid can also be used as a self-administered survey instrument or as an instrument that is objectively completed by others who know and observe the group leader. The instrument can be scored and a Leadership Skills Profile based on the scores can be prepared. When used as a self-assessment survey, the individual is required to indicate how much of each skill he or she thinks that he or she possesses by placing an x in the relevant box after each attribute. The possible total score for each skill is 4. For the questioning skill,

Table 9.3.

Group Facilitation and Leading Skills/Rating	How Much of Each Attribute Do You Possess?	How Much of Each Attribute Do You Wish to Acquire and How?	Feedback, Comments and Discussion
Blocking			
Confronting			
Cuing			
Disclosing			
Energizing			
Interpreting			
Linking			
Questioning			
Reflecting Feeling			
Reframing			
Rephrasing			
Suggesting			
Summarizing			
Supporting			

Table 9.4.

Group Facilitation and Leading Skills/Rating	None 0	Little 1	Some 2	Much 3	Very Much 4	Score	Comments
Blocking		x				1	
Confronting	x					0	
Cuing		x				1	
Disclosing				x		3	
Energizing					x	4	
Interpreting		x				1	
Linking	x					0	
Questioning						3.5	
• Open-ended questions				x			
• Close-ended questions					x		
Reflecting Feeling				x		3	
Reframing			x			2	
Rephrasing				x		3	
Suggesting					x	4	
Summarizing		x				1	
Supporting				x		3	
Total						29.5	2.07 on the 4 point scale. Skill potential of .52

each of the two dimensions: open-ended questions and close-ended questions, receives a separate score. The questioning skill total score is the sum of these two dimensions divided by 2. The possible total score for all of the skills combined and for the instrument as a whole is 14 x 4 = 56.

Group Leadership Skills Profile

The example presented in table 9.4 and figure 9.2, shows an individual who scores highest on the leadership skills of energizing and suggesting with a score of 4 each, and scores lowest on the leadership skills of confronting and linking with a score of 0 each. The leadership skills of blocking, cuing, interpreting and summarizing were also quite low with a score of 1 each on the scale. The person's overall score on a scale from 0 to 56 is 29.5. This profile indicates someone who needs much more group leadership skill development overall with strong emphasis on those areas identified as being very weak.

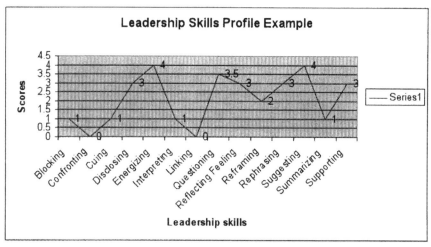

Figure 9.2.

The individual's leadership skill potential which is the total skill score on the four point scale, 2.07 divided by 4 which is .52 out of a possible 1. The goal is to reach a leadership skill potential score of 1.

CO-LEADERSHIP CONSIDERATIONS

There are some instances during which two individuals co-leading a group may be desirable. Usually one person is the group leader and takes the lead role and the other person is the co-leader and assumes a supporting leadership role. One such instance is in a situation in which the co-leader is in training and learning how to lead and facilitate groups from a more experienced group leader. In this case the co-leader is, in effect, being supervised and mentored by the group leader and may play a minimal role in actually co-leading and more of an observer and learner role. Over time the individual takes on more of a true co-leadership role.

There are instances in which the co-leader is experienced and is invited by the group leader to bring special knowledge and expertise to complement the knowledge and skills of the group leader. In other instances the co-leader may be assigned to co-lead a group by virtue of work requirements or may seek out an opportunity to co-lead the group based on interest or desire to serve. In situations with an experienced co-leader the coordination and synchronization is essential and the two group leaders have to be careful, mutually respectful and synergistic. It is important for the two group leaders to have a pre-group planning meeting and to have regular debriefing and processing meetings after each group session.

In providing feedback to group members and in responding to questions and requests for guidance from group members, the group leaders must be careful not to confuse group members with contradictory messages. Depending on the type of group, the two group leaders may express differing opinions on issues. But even then this has to be done in a manner that is mutually respectful and sensitive and responsive to the group as a whole, keeping in mind the purpose and goals of the group. The integrity of the group process and the best interest of group members must be placed ahead of the individual or ego needs of the co-leaders.

In closed groups, such as counseling and therapy groups, just as group members are selected before the group begins and new members are not allowed to join the group after the group has started, so too a co-leader should be selected before the group begins and should not join the group after it has started. This is to protect the feelings of comfort, trust and confidence that the group members have established among themselves and with the group leadership and to minimize disruption of the group process. In open groups such as in support groups, just as group membership can be fluid and flexible, the group leadership may be more flexible in terms of when co-leaders may join. However, there still must be responsible and sensitive changes in group leadership. In all situations where there is co-leadership it is expected that group members will be informed about the nature of the co-leadership relationship as well as the qualifications and backgrounds of the co-leaders.

Chapter Ten

Teams

A team may be viewed as a work group that functions within clearly defined parameters, with each member expected to work well with other team members to accomplish the team's goals. Some teams function effectively in achieving the stated goals and other teams do not and may fail to accomplish stated goals or be less efficient in accomplishing goals. Most teams would like to be effective and increasing a team's effectiveness is often the goal of team building and team training sessions.

EFFECTIVE TEAM CHARACTERISTICS

There are several team characteristics that have been identified as being important to effective teams. These are:

- motivated and dedicated team members,
- effective leadership,
- clearly articulated purpose and goals that are shared by team members,
- clearly identified roles and responsibilities,
- workable action plan,
- process for resolving conflict,
- consensus decision making process,
- respect for each member's opinions and ideas,
- diverse knowledge and skills that support team's mission, purpose and goals,
- effective communication structures
- effective use of power bases by team members

- good balance between task orientation and people orientation, and
- adequate attention to content and process.

Motivated and Dedicated Team Members

In forming a team it is important to identify and select team members who are committed to the purpose and goals of the team. Team members need to become and remain fully motivated to perform the tasks that they are assigned or agree to perform as members of the team. There are times during a team's work that members may become discouraged or demoralized and lose the optimism about the team's ability to accomplish its goals. It is important for the team's leader to use his or her leadership skills of energizing, inspiring and motivating team members. Teams cannot succeed, or cannot succeed as well as they should, if members of that team lose their dedication and are not fully motivated.

Effective Leadership

An effective team requires effective leadership that combines the attributes and skills that were discussed in chapter seven. The team leader may be assigned, nominated or elected by team members or may volunteer for the position. The process by which the team leader is identified sometimes influences his or her relationship to team members and, in turn, his or her effectiveness. The effective team leader develops and cultivates a viable relationship with team members and creates a positive climate in which the members of the team can work successfully together.

Clearly Articulated Purpose and Goals That Are Shared By Team Members

Every team should have a clearly stated purpose and related achievable and measurable goals. The very first order of business on any team must be to ensure that each team member knows, understands and supports the team's purpose and the related goals. A team's success is determined by the extent to which the team is able to fulfill its purpose and accomplish its goals. The purpose and goals provide direction and serve as benchmarks to monitor and assess how well the team is doing. Having total buy-in by team members to the purpose and goals is important and necessary for team success. Some may argue that total buy-in is not always possible or desirable. However, one uncommitted and unmotivated member can sabotage, hinder and hurt the team's progress. It is important to know how committed every team member is to the team's work and address and alleviate any concerns and resistance that the team members may have. In some instances, when every other attempt to break a team member's resistance or to motivate and energize a team member fails, that team member may have to be asked to resign or be removed from the team.

Clearly Identified Roles and Responsibilities

Team members need to be clear about what their expected roles and responsibilities are in order for them to be energized and motivated to participate in the team's work. When roles and responsibilities are not clear, there can be confusion, unnecessary duplication of effort and inefficient use of time and resources. Team members can also become demoralized, disillusioned and disinterested if they begin to feel that their skills and talents are unutilized or underutilized.

Workable Action Plan

Effective teams usually work from a blue print for success in the form of a workable action plan. The action plan is designed with input, gathered in one way or another, from key stakeholders who may be impacted by the decision or product that the team is working to develop. The plan serves as a GPS that includes the team's goals or destination, the strategies that will lead to the accomplishment of the goals, timelines for achieving objectives that are tied to the goals, tasks to be performed, and clear roles and responsibilities among team members for completing tasks. Such an action plan gives the team direction, solidifies its purpose and helps to maintain interest and momentum among team members.

Process for Resolving Conflict

Most teams experience conflict as members work to produce the best result in a free and open process with diverse input from members. A diversity of ideas, which at times may be in conflict, can be healthy and useful for the development of the team. As noted in the discussion on the stages of group development in chapter two, conflict in groups is viewed as a positive element in the group's progression toward getting the work done. However, conflict without a workable solution does not serve the group's interest. A team should have an established protocol for addressing and resolving conflicts as they arise. In some types of groups the group leader uses leadership skills such as confronting, suggesting and summarizing to help the group develop consensus, resolve the conflict and move the group forward. On teams, which are essentially work groups, leadership skills combined with a clear decision making process, such as the use of consensus, seem to be most effective in resolving conflicts and helping to get the work done.

Decision Making Process

The process that the team uses to make decisions is important to the team's success. On some teams, an autocratic decision making process is used in which the team leader decides and the team implements what the leader decides. This approach to decision making may work in some situations and may be deemed to be most efficient and much less time consuming than other approaches in those specific situations. For example, in the military there is not much room for any other form of decision making than what the military prescribes in order to build a cohesive and unified force. However, in most other situations, this approach is likely to result in more dissatisfied team members, decreased team morale, reduced team member commitment to team goals and depressed motivation. There is a variation to the autocratic approach that may be called a "modified autocratic" approach in which the team leader decides from among a set of decisions that the team members may suggest. In this approach, there is team input but the final decision is the team leader's decision. The effect of this approach is likely to be similar to the autocratic approach given the fact that the team leader still has veto power over decisions and retains the final decision-making authority.

There are more democratic approaches to decision making that may take longer but that have more positive consequences for the team. One such approach is the typical majority rule approach in which decisions are decided by majority vote after alternatives are brainstormed and discussed. The advantage of majority vote is that each member is heard and gets to contribute ideas during the brainstorming process. The disadvantage is that when the votes are counted, the team members in the majority become winners and the team members in the minority become losers. Losers often do not like to lose and may resist the decisions which they perceive the majority is "imposing" on the team. The result may be a small group of team members, who may passively, or may be not so passively, resist majority rule and who may decide not to invest fully in the team's work.

The other democratic approach is one that uses decision making by consensus. In the consensus approach there is a brainstorming process in which all team members suggest ideas and make the case for their ideas, but unlike majority rule, there is no voting. Instead, the ideas that are advanced during brainstorming are evaluated according to certain criteria and rank ordered based on those criteria. These criteria may include: relevance, feasibility, plausibility, cost-benefit, time, legality and ethics, consistency with organizational policy and procedures, and likelihood of controversy. These criteria are explained and discussed below in the special section on consensus. The consensus process demonstrates respect for each member's opinions and ideas and eliminates the zero sum game perception that is inherent in the winners-losers, majority-rule paradigm.

Diverse Knowledge and Skills that Support the Team's Purpose and Goals

The interests of a team are best served when the team is comprised of team members who bring a diverse set of knowledge and skills to the team's work. A team whose members are totally homogeneous with respect to their skill sets or knowledge is a team that lacks originality, creativity and innovative thinking. For some tasks and in some situations homogeneity and strict conformity to a rigid predetermined formula may be required. Assembly line tasks and military units are examples where diversity of ideas, originality and creativity may not be as important as conformity and adherence to preset standards or expectations. In most cases, however, team diversity in skills and knowledge is an asset. This is no more obvious than on sports teams that require players with a variety of skills to play in different positions. Not every player on a football team needs to be a quarter back and not every player on a soccer team needs to be a goal keeper. The team is best served when players are assembled because of the diversity they bring to the team and are able to blend and orchestrate that diversity into a winning combination for the team.

Effective Communication Structures

In chapter four, different kinds of communication structures were described and discussed. Communication structures range from highly centralized, in which one person or authority controls communication among members of a group, to highly decentralized, in which all members of a group communicate freely with one another. On teams, the degree to which communication is centralized or decentralized is often tied to the degree to which the leadership of teams and the decision making process are autocratic or democratic. On most teams it is most helpful for the communication structure to be free and open with team members able to communicate directly with one another. However, there are some situations in which the protocols that govern how the team functions may call for communication to be structured in a more centralized way. Team members usually appreciate being part of the communication structure and having their voices heard and respected as a part of the decision-making process. The manner in which team members communicate with one another is an important indicator of how cohesive the team is and the likelihood that the team will accomplish its goals.

Effective Use of Power Bases by Team Members

The more empowered team members feel, the greater the likelihood that they will participate fully and completely in the work of the team. In chapter six, the sources from which group members derive power or the bases on which they establish their power are discussed. It is very important that each member of a team becomes aware of, know and fully understand the power bases and his or her strongest and weakest sources of power. Knowing one's strongest power bases enables the individual to maximize that source of power on the team and to contribute as productively as possible to the work of the team. On the other hand knowing one's weakest power bases can lead the individual to find ways to increase and enhance those sources of power on the team thereby strengthening the individual's position of influence on the team.

Balance Between Task Orientation and People Orientation

Striking a balance between an emphasis on getting the task done and an emphasis on the needs and feelings of team members who are expected to get the work done is important to the effectiveness of a team. Some teams tend to be so focused on the task that team members feel that they are treated as robots, with their needs and feelings neglected. On the other hand, some teams seem to spend so much time and effort on the needs and feelings of team members that the task that the team is expected to address does not get accomplished in a timely fashion. There is a point at which both task completion and team member needs can be adequately and satisfactorily addressed simultaneously and finding that balance enhances the team's effectiveness.

Adequate Attention to Content and Process

Just as the effective team needs to have a balance between its task orientation and its people orientation, it also needs to have a balance between the content of what is being addressed and the process by which it is addressing the content. In other words, the team has to be concerned in a balanced way with "what" it does and "how" it does it. The content of the group's work often receives more attention than the process by which the work gets done. This is the case because most often the team is judged by the product that is delivered at the end of the process which is the content in completed and finished form. However, the process is important because how the team works, including the interpersonal dynamics among team members, determines how the content takes shape and the quality of the finished product.

MORE ABOUT CONSENSUS

As mentioned earlier, consensus is a form of democratic decision making that does not involve voting and does not depend on majority rule. There is no zero sum game. It avoids winners and losers. Consensus means that we are thinking through the problem and arriving at a solution together. There are several rules that should guide the process of consensus. These are:

- All team members take part in the decision making process from brainstorming decision alternatives to selecting the best decision alternative.
- All team members make a concerted effort to understand the opinions, views and suggestions of others.
- All team members with ideas to share should have an equal opportunity to share their ideas and suggestions.
- The team should arrive at decisions that meet the expectations of all team members based on group discussion and the collective input of team members.
- Following discussion, decision alternatives are ranked based on established criteria and all group members support the ranking of decision alternatives.
- The decision alternative that is ranked first is the first to be implemented and given a fair chance to work. If that decision does not work, then the team goes to the next decision alternative and repeats that process until the workable decision is found.

The essence of consensus may be summed up as:

"I believe that I understand your position
I believe that you understand my position
I will support the position of the group, whether I agree or not, because it was reached fairly and openly." (Wynn, & Guditus, 1984, p. 43).

Criteria for Evaluating Decision Alternatives

- *Relevance:* In evaluating alternatives that result from brainstorming among team members, how relevant a suggested alternative course of action is to the team's purpose and goals should be considered. Not all decisions that sound good may be relevant. A relevant decision is one that would advance the work of the team.

- *Feasibility:* Some relevant decisions may not be possible to implement. There may be obstacles to practically taking the decision from the idea or concept stage to the implementation stage. Feasible decisions are those that are practical given the situation and the circumstances in which the decision is to be implemented.
- *Plausibility:* How reasonable a decision alternative may be has to be considered when selecting the best alternative. A reasonable decision is one that does not impose undue hardship or make excessive demands on those who are expected to implement the decision. Therefore, a feasible decision may not be plausible. For example, if a team has a project to complete and to submit for evaluation by their peers and by the professor, it may be feasible for the team to work on a project that examines the effects of sleeplessness on group cohesion. This may require the members of a group to stay awake all night and then work on solving a problem the following day. The decision to select this topic for presentation is feasible. It is doable. It is practical. However, it is not plausible. It places an undue hardship on the individuals who must go sleepless all night.
- *Cost-Benefit*: Cost-benefit considerations should guide the selection of decisions that have costs associated with them. The monetary and non-monetary costs associated with a decision should be considered in relation to the benefits that may accrue from implementing that decision. Those decisions in which the costs of implementation outweigh the benefits should probably not be selected.
- *Time:* The amount of time that is required to implement a decision alternative must be considered. Some decisions may require more time than is available to implement them well. The team must be concerned with the most effective use of time and how to utilize the available time to get the job done efficiently and well.
- *Legality and Ethics:* Any decision alternative that the team decides to accept and implement should be legal and ethical. The decision should pass muster when held up against the legal and ethical standards of practice.
- *Consistency with Established Organizational Policies and Procedures:* The established policies and procedures of the organization in which the team is functioning have to be considered and the selected decision alternative should be consistent with those policies and procedures as long as they are legal and ethical.
- *Likelihood of Controversy*: Decision alternatives that are likely to stir up controversy and result in disaffection, hurt feelings and disunity may be counterproductive and should probably be avoided unless the team's task is

to shake up the system, and bring about needed changes in the system. Even so, this has to be done carefully, and with a plan in mind to pick up the pieces and put them together again into a workable and viable functional unit.

MOTIVATING TEAM MEMBERS TO CARE

Sometimes on teams, some members may take a longer time to become fully on board with the purpose and goals of the team. There are six steps that can be taken to motivate and inspire fuller participation in the teams work. Each step begins with the letter "I" so this approach to motivating team members may be called the "six-I approach." The six steps are presented in the grid shown in table 10.1.

For example, assume that a team has been formed to provide psychological and emotional relief to the fishermen and their families on the gulf coast who have been affected by the oil spill. The team will spend at least six months in the area living among and interacting with the fishermen and their families, offering psychological and emotional support. This requires that team members be prepared to make the sacrifice to travel to the gulf coast region and dedicate six months of their time. The issue is how to interest and motivate a large enough number of individuals to join the team and to become highly motivated to do this job. According to the "six-I" approach the following steps will be followed:

Step 1: Introduce: The proposed work with the families in the gulf region will be introduced to prospective team members. The introduction will include information about the gulf spill, the facts about the amount oil in the gulf and the impact on fishing in the gulf. This information will help to raise awareness about the extent to which many families depend on fishing for their livelihood and of the possible damage to the fishing industry there. Introduction may be used as a recruitment step in the team building process.

Table 10.1.

Introduce	Inform	Impress	Instill	Invite	Involve
Consciousness Raising: Provide background information to raise awareness.	Provide sufficient information to enhance understanding.	Give Reason to care.	Give a local imperative. Explain why it is important to the people involved.	Extend an invitation to get involved. Say: "Let's see what we can do?"	Provide an opportunity for action.

Step 2: Inform: Additional and more detailed information will be presented on the technical aspects of the spill, the efforts to clean up the gulf and the possible long-term impact on the lives of the people in the gulf region. This information will increase team members understanding of the gravity of the issue and may serve to orient team members to key concerns among the people in the gulf region.

Step 3: Impress: Now that team members have factual information that has raised their awareness and increased their understanding of the issues involved, the question may still remain, "why should I care about the oil spill and its impact on people in the gulf region?" First, there is a humanitarian consideration involved. These are people who could lose their livelihoods and whose lives can be permanently altered and devastated. The team's work can help to buffer the psychological and emotional impact. Also, there is a larger national economic impact that could affect not just the people in the gulf but that could affect the nation. Without a return to fishing in the gulf, there could be a ripple effect directly and indirectly on related businesses. This could conceivably slow the national economic recovery. Therefore, supporting the families in the gulf by maintaining their confidence and self-esteem would increase their resilience to be able to bounce back and to rebuild the economy of the region. Team members need to be given a reason to care.

Step 4: Instill: Given the humanitarian concerns as well as the national implications for the disaster in the gulf, people from across the country need to mobilize to help. The team's proposed efforts to provide psychological and emotional support is very much needed given the scarcity of such services for families and the tendency for mental health needs to be overlooked or treated as secondary to the more visible economic and physical impact during such disasters. It is imperative that the team members become involved.

Step 5: Invite: Each team member is being invited to become involved and to be a part of this extremely important humanitarian effort. Every person's input and support is needed and valued so "let's see what we can do as a team." Each team member has an opportunity to consider how he or she may best serve the effort.

Step 6: Involve: Each team member now has a clear idea of how he or she can be involved with specific tasks to be performed in preparation for going to the gulf region and for after arriving in the gulf region. Roles and responsibilities are clearly explained. For example, a group member's role might involve organizing and coordinating housing for team members while they are in the gulf region.

Activity #22: Team Assessment

Team members are invited to assess their team's effectiveness by completing a Team Effectiveness Scale. The scale includes the elements discussed above as key ingredients of effective teams. Team members use the information provided above to think about, reflect on and discuss the extent to which the team possesses each of the elements using a five-point likert-type scale ranging from strongly disagree =1 disagree to strongly agree = 5. The scale is completed together as a team to facilitate discussion among team members. This approach allows for team members to share their perspectives on how the team is functioning and to hear and understand other team members' perspectives.

Directions:

On a scale from 1 to 5 with 1= strongly disagree (SD); 2=disagree (D); 3=neither disagree or agree (N); 4= agree; (A) 5=strongly agree (SA) indicate the extent to which you disagree or agree that your team has the following important elements of an effective team.

Table 10.2.

The Team Possesses:	Strongly Disagree (SD)	Disagree (D)	Neither Agree or Disagree (N)	Agree (A)	Strongly Agree (SA)
Motivated and Dedicated Team Members					
Effective Leadership					
Clearly Articulated Purpose and Goals That Are Shared By Team Members					
Clearly Identified Roles and Responsibilities					
Workable Action Plan					
Process for Resolving Conflict					
Consensus Decision Making Process					
Respect for Each Member's Opinions and Ideas					
Diverse Knowledge and Skills That Support Team's Mission, Purpose and Goals					
Effective Communication Structures					
Effective Use of Power Bases By Team Members					
Balance Between Task and People Orientations					
Total Score					

Chapter Eleven

Assessing and Evaluating the Group Process and Its Effects: Evaluating a Psycho-educational Group Process

Knowing whether or not a group is functioning well, meeting its goals and having the desired effects for group members and other target constituents is very important. Unfortunately many times the group process and its effects go un-assessed and the group's impact remains unknown. There are several ways or methods to assess a group's effectiveness and impact, ranging from using relatively simple procedures to using more complex evaluation designs. The simplicity or complexity of the methods used would depend on: the nature of the group, the purpose and goals of the group, the expected outcomes, the audience for whom the evaluation is conducted and the extent to which the generalizability of the evaluation results is an important consideration. The methods used may involve the use of qualitative or narrative data only, quantitative or numerical data only or a combination of both. Some approaches to collecting data on the group process are discussed below.

DATA COLLECTION METHODS AND MEASURES

Journals

Perhaps, the simplest and most direct way to assess a group's process and its effects is through group members' journals. Journaling is a qualitative method of collecting data or information about the group process and its effects. Journals are not simply a retelling of events that transpire in the group. A journal is not a diary. Journals are much more substantive, reflective and evaluative. As noted in chapter six, journals are reflective narratives in which the group member describes and discusses key and significant aspects of the group process and how that member participates in and is affected by interactions among group members. The member comments on the group climate and group leadership and shares increasingly deeper reflections about how the individual is impacted by the experience over time.

Interviews

Interviews provide an opportunity for the evaluator to collect information directly from individual group members regarding the group process and its effects. The interview may be unstructured, during which the interviewer may have some prepared questions as general guidelines for the interview. He or she may allow the group member to help frame the direction in which the interview goes. The questions flow organically from the question and answer dynamic of the interview process. The interview may also be structured, during which the interviewer has a set of prepared and pre-coded questions that frame the interview. In both structured and unstructured interviews open and close-ended questions may be used, but there is likely to be more open-ended questions used in the unstructured interview format and more close-ended questions used in the structured interview format. Also, the structured interview format is more likely to use a combination of qualitative and quantitative data (for example, checklist or rating scale) whereas the unstructured interview is more likely to use only qualitative data.

Focus Groups

The focus group may be sometimes viewed as an interview with several individuals all at once. However, the focus group is much more than a collective interview. It is a structured conversation with several participants during which a set of prepared questions focus attention and gather information about aspects of a key issue. It also allows the emotions involved in the consideration of the issue to be seen and felt among the focus group participants. Capturing the energy and dynamic among the participants and incorporating process as well as the content in the analysis is important. Focus groups rely mostly on qualitative data. The number of participants in a focus group varies but should be small enough to be manageable and to encourage universal participation and large enough to provide diverse opinions and ideas on the issue. As noted in chapter three, the guidelines for the optimum size of an effective group, including a focus group, is 5–10.

Un-standardized and Standardized Measures:
Surveys, Questionnaires and Rating Scales

In some instances, data on the group process and its effects may be collected through surveys, questionnaires and rating scales, on which participants are invited to provide a judgment about aspects of the group process. These instruments, as they are called in the assessment and evaluation literature, are usually comprised of a number of items made up of statements to which the participant responds either on a two point scale such as "yes" or "no"/ "true" or "false" or on a scale with a larger range of responses such as on a likert scale which is normally a five point scale such as : "strongly disagree"= 1; "disagree" = 2; "neither disagree nor agree" = 3; "agree" = 4; "strongly agree" = 5. A total score is computed for each participant then the total scores for all participants are added together and divided by the number of participants to get a mean score. The mean score is often used as the numerical value of the group's effectiveness. Un-standardized measures are those that have not been normed or standardized using a representative sample of individuals, therefore the data generated cannot be compared to a normative sample. Standardized measures on the other hand have been normed and standardized using a representative sample and the data generated can be compared to a normative sample.

APPLYING EVALUATION METHODS TO A
PSYCHO-EDUCATIONAL GROUP

Overview and Background

In this section the evaluation of a psycho-educational group process called the Interest Achievement and Motivation (I AM) process is described. Before specifically addressing how the evaluation was conducted, an overview of the I AM group process is first provided as a context for understanding the evaluation. The French Philosopher, Descartes noted: "I think therefore I am." This can be interpreted as, the fact that I can think validates my existence and confirms the power that I have as an individual through the use of my mind. Students need to know that they have the capacity to think, to use their brains to achieve great things if they set their minds to it. Educators are encouraged to consider the fact that each and every child has the capacity to think, learn, and to succeed academically with proper and effective instruction, guidance and support.

Many educators face the daily challenge of motivating their students to learn, to show interest in school work, and to achieve to the best of their potential.

One of the major motivational blocks to high academic achievement is negative academic self-concept, and students' doubts about their capabilities, efficacy, and worth as learners (McCombs & Whisler, 1997). Students' beliefs about themselves and about their general academic abilities significantly influence their interest, their achievement, and their motivation to learn. (Madden, 1997). Educators continue to struggle with the issue of how to enhance students' positive academic self-concepts in order to increase their interest, motivation, and achievement in school.

The purpose of the study was to examine the effects of a psycho-educational group called the Interest, Achievement, and Motivation (I AM) group. The group is designed to address the problem of students' underachievement by endeavoring to increase students' academic self-concept and change their approach to learning. It seeks to build students' confidence and belief in their potential to be successful in school. It assumes that an increase in academic self-confidence and academic self-efficacy is likely to also increase students' success-oriented behaviors and improve their academic performance. Enhancing student's achievement motivation is at the heart of the group process.

Motivation

Motivation has been defined as "the desire to achieve a goal that has value for the individual" (Linskie, 1997). *Achievement motivation* is a person's internal desire to succeed and is generally accompanied by a need to avoid failure and an effort on the person's part to be successful (Boggiano & Pittman, 1992; Jegede, 1997). A positive relationship between achievement motivation and academic performance has been indicated in past studies (Jegede, 1997). This is the reason that it is an important concept that is stressed in the "I AM" group process.

Self-esteem

In addition to achievement motivation, the positive relationship between self-esteem and academic performance has also been supported by the literature (Meece, Blumenfeld, & Hoyle, 1988; Nichols, 1996; Nichols and Miller, 1994; Nichols and Utesch, 1998). *Self-esteem* is defined by Woolfolk (1995) as how we evaluate our self-concept and the value we place on our behaviors and capabilities. Students with high self-esteem (or, positive self-concept) are more likely to be successful academically, have better attitudes toward and greater interest in school, more positive classroom behavior, and popularity amongst peers (Cauley & Tyler, 1989; Marsh, 1990; Mecalfe, 1981; Nichols and Utesch, 1998; Reynolds, 1980).

McCombs and Whisler (1997) discussed how negative self-concept and feelings of insecurity about one's efficacy can thwart a child's enthusiasm and normal intrinsic motivation to learn. Alderman (1990) noted that whether students attribute their successes in school to external versus internal factors (e.g. poor studying versus poor intelligence) has an effect on motivation. If a child internally believes that he or she is not smart or capable, motivation to succeed and school achievement can drop. The promotion of positive self-concept is an integral part of the "I AM" group process and is one of the dependent variables being examined in this study.

Goal Setting

One of the concepts addressed in the "I AM" group process is goal-setting or, rather, how to plan long and short-term goals. Madden (1997) investigated how 126 elementary teachers motivated their students to do effective goal setting. Important conclusions made from this study include:

1. "Students work more diligently on self-made goals than from the expectations of other."
2. "Children who feel self-efficacy (competence or power) in reaching goals show effort and persistence."
3. "Children who know that they can reach their highest goals are more motivated to work toward them."
4. Children are more motivated to work toward goals they can obtain quickly. (Madden 1997).

Thus, the "I AM" group process stresses the idea of creating personal goals and through the promotion of positive self-concept, it is hoped that they will feel efficacious in achieving their goals.

Teacher Expectations and Support

Wentzel (1990) examined the relationship of peer, parent, and teacher relations to student motivation. In regards to teacher support, the factor examined in this study, Wentzel (1990) found that it was a positive predictor of school interest and social responsibility goals. According to Piers (1984), children's self reports (such as the Piers-Harris Scale used in this study) have not always significantly corresponded with teacher ratings. However, later studies have confirmed the positive relationship between students' self-concept and academic achievement and teachers' expectations (Good & Brophy, 1987; Haynes, 1996; Madden, 1997; Wentzel, 1990).

Therefore, a teacher school behavior rating form was prepared for this study to evaluate how teachers expect their students to perform in school. The relationship between self-concept (as measured by the Piers-Harris Children's Self-Concept Scale) and teacher expectations (as measured by the teacher rating form) was examined in this study.

One way that is intended to bolster positive self-concept in the "I AM" group and used in this study is to recite affirmations. According to Canfield and Wells (1994), an affirmation "asserts a desired condition or objective as though it were already a reality" (p. 234). An affirmation has six essential components: "It's personal, it's positive, it's specific, it's visual, it's present tense, and it's emotional." (Canfield & Wells, 1994, p. 234). An example of an affirmation might be, "I do very well at solving word problems in math!"

Social Skills

It was mentioned earlier that peer, parent, and teacher support have important effects on student self-concept, motivation and achievement. One roadblock to support on any of these levels can be poor social skills and behaviors. In a review study of social skills interventions conducted by Zaragoza, Vaughn, and McIntosh (1991), students with behavior problems are more likely to be rejected by their peers and targeted for teacher reprimand than by peers who behave normally. Thus, the I AM group process address the issue of proper social behavior. In each classroom, there tends to be some students who can benefit from lessons in proper social skills.

One program similar to the "I AM" group, that focuses on motivating students and bolstering positive self-concept is Hootstein's (1996) RISE (Relevance, Interest, Satisfaction, and Expectations) model for motivating at-risk students to learn. It emphasizes concepts previously alluded to, such as use of positive self-talk (affirmations), realistic and personal goal-setting in order to gain a sense of accomplishment, satisfaction, and efficacy, and teacher support to bolster motivation (Hootstein, 1996). All of these concepts are important components in the I AM group process.

The "I AM" process is similar to the RISE model in that the "I AM" group also looks at students' interest and students' beliefs about their ability to suc-ceed. Additionally, the evaluation study of the I AM process being reported in this chapter also looks at students who are at-risk (by virtue of poverty, neighborhood safety, low self-esteem, boredom in school, poor health, etc.) of not achieving to their full potential in school. Students who are bored due to the lack of a connection they see between their learning and outside lives may be perceived as unmotivated when they are simply yearning for more real-life relevant learning material (Hootstein, 1996). Davis Street Elementary School in New Haven, Connecticut where the implementation of the "I AM" group process occurred and was evaluated for this study has been a target for the Comer School Development Program, a program that improves school climate and promotes violence prevention, because it was defined as a school with at-risk students (Haynes, 1996).

Another example of a motivation group model is Magliocca's and Robinson's (1991) "I Can" strategy for promoting self-confidence. Magliocca and Robinson (1991) emphasize immediately identifying and praising positive behavior, breaking problems down into smaller steps (addressed in the I AM problem-solving class session), and encouraging risk-taking. For example, a student may be praised immediately for raising her hand before speaking. Students are told that it's alright to take a risk and make a mistake because everyone makes mistakes and can learn from those mistakes. (Magliocca & Robinson, 1991). These ideas and concepts were utilized during the I AM group process.

Structure of the I AM Group Process

The "I AM" group process is an eight week program of developmental guidance lessons for a whole class of students. It can also be conducted as a series of small group sessions with a similar curriculum of developmental guidance lessons. Each group session is designed to emphasize a particular theme in terms of social skills, school interest, achievement, and motivation. Affirmations are recited at the beginning of each session to help students internalize positive messages about themselves such as "I am a good person" and "I will succeed." The goals of the group are to:

1. engender a positive sense of self among students and to encourage a positive belief in their potential to achieve at high levels in school.
2. support and reinforce achievement-related behaviors among students.
3. encourage and support positive attitudes towards school and work among students.
4. increase students' achievement motivation and influence their academic performance.
5. reinforce prosocial values, attitudes and behaviors.

The weekly group sessions during the eight weeks are outlined below.

Week One/Session One: During week one, the I AM group process was introduced to the classes and rapport was established. The use and purpose of the positive affirmations were explained. The purpose of the group process was explained as being to help students feel better about themselves and about their academic potential, and to foster prosocial and goal-oriented behaviors.

The pretest on the Behavior and Intellectual and School Status subscales of the Piers-Harris Self-Concept Scale was administered to students. Teachers also completed the pre-test on the teacher rating form.

Week Two/Session Two: During week two, the group process began with the positive affirmations. The theme for session two was goal setting. Students were taught how to set and achieve long-term and short-term goals. They described themselves as they might see themselves when they grow up. Students were given a ditto sheet with footsteps so they could define the steps they needed to take to achieve their goals.

Week Three/Session Three: During week three, the group process began with positive affirmations. The theme for session three was problem solving and each student received a handout with general information about how to solve problems. Students were explained the game of chess and were taught to play the game using the opportunity of playing the game to emphasize thinking and strategizing in problem solving.

Week Four/Session Four: During week four, the group process began with positive affirmations. The theme for session four was social skills training and assertiveness. A video titled: "How to Say 'No' Without Losing Your Friends" was shown. The video provided some information and training on assertiveness. After watching the video, there was a discussion on how to deal with peer pressure and the group facilitators answered questions from students, based on their personal experiences, about how to be assertive in various situations.

Week Five/Session Five: During week five, the group process began with positive affirmations. The theme for session five was school attendance, doing well on class assignments, homework, and test-taking. Students were given handouts on this topic and discussed the importance of regular and punctual attendance and productive study/work habits. It was during this week that we had the principal come in to give a motivational speech to the class-groups about their potential, the importance of a good education, and to offer encouraging praise. This allowed the students to see the principal in a role other than that of an authority figure.

Week Six/Session Six: During week six, the group process began with positive affirmations. The theme for session six was respecting the feelings of others and the importance of maintaining positive social relationships with others, including respecting the authority of adults. Vignettes about typical social situations were presented and appropriate ways to act in those situations were discussed. There were also discussions about how students feel when they are laughed at, made fun of, or praised and recognized for the good things they do.

Week Seven/Session Seven: During week seven, the group process began with positive affirmations. The theme for session seven was getting in touch with one's own emotions and how to communicate those emotions. Students were encouraged to express their feelings in appropriate ways and we discussed the importance of communicating hurt feelings as opposed to acting out with aggression. Classical music was played and students were invited to draw or write how they felt that day.

Week Eight/Session Eight: During week eight the group process began with positive affirmations. Prior to the graduation ceremony, students discussed the "I AM" group process and how it affected them. The Behavior Self-Concept subscale and Intellectual and School Status subscale from the Piers-Harris Self-Concept Scale were administered. The graduation ceremony was held and students were presented with a certificate of completion for participating in the "I AM" group process.

Evaluation

The question addressed in the evaluation study was "what effects does the "I AM" group process have on students' behavioral self-concept, academic self-concept and teachers' ratings of students' general school behaviors? For this study, the "I AM" group process was used in the fourth grade classes at Davis Street Elementary School in New Haven, Connecticut. The rationale for using fourth grade students was based on the behavioral and academic challenges that existed among the fourth graders during that period of time. The school work became significantly more challenging for the fourth graders. The fourth grade is one of the transitional grades (along with fifth grade) between elementary and middle school. The issue of readiness for the middle school experience is an important issue (Ames, 1994). Additionally, peer groups begin to exert much stronger (and possible negative) influences on attitudes and behavior during the fourth grade (Hilliard & Lomotey, 1990; Comer, 1988; Rossi, 1994).

It was hypothesized that the "I AM" group process would have a positive impact on students' behavioral self-concept and academic self-concept (as measured by the Piers-Harris Self-Concept Scale) and on teachers' ratings of school-related behaviors (as measured by the teacher rating form designed specifically for this study. The independent variable was the "I AM" group process. There were eight sessions per group process which addressed the following topics: focus on the self as a unique person, goal-setting and achieving goals, school attendance and behavior, class work and homework habits, achievement motivation and test-taking skills, social problem solving skills, academic and social self-confidence, and the conclusion (an integration of what was learned) with the presentation of reward certificates

The dependent variables of behavioral self-concept, and intellectual and school status, were measured with the Behavior (16 items) and Intellectual and School Status (17 items) subscales of the Piers-Harris Children's Self-

Concept Scale. The other dependent variable, teacher assessment of students' school attitude and performance was measured by the teacher rating scale.

Participants

All students in three fourth grade classrooms at Davis Elementary School were exposed to the "I AM" group process. There were approximately 20-22 students in each classroom. Forty eight of these fourth grade students received parental consent to participate in the evaluation study. The "I AM" psycho-educational group process was incorporated into the weekly developmental guidance schedule of the three classes. Most of the students in this research study were of African American descent. Within the total sample, there were three Caucasian students and four Hispanic students. The ages of participants ranged from age 8 to 10 years and the average age of the participants was 10 years.

Measuring Self-Concept and Teacher Expectations

This study used two dimensions from the Piers-Harris Children's Self-Concept Scale (1969) a self-report scale to measure self-concept before and after the "I AM" group process (See Appendices B-1 and B-2). Specifically, the Behavior and the Intellectual and School Status scales were used. The Piers Harris Self-Concept Scale was designed for use with students aged 8 to 18 years and was appropriate for use with the fifth grade students in the study. The Behavior scale "reflects the extent to which the child admits or denies problematic behaviors" (Piers, 1984). The Intellectual and School Status scale "reflects the child's self-assessment of his or her abilities with respect to intellectual and academic tasks, including general satisfaction with school and future expectations" (Piers, 1984). As mentioned previously, student behavior, self- perceptions about abilities, attitudes toward school and expectations and goals all have an effect on achievement motivation.

Reliability is high for the Piers-Harris with internal consistency scores ranging from .88 to .93 and test-retest reliability ranging from .62 to .96 (Page and Chandler, 1994). One possible weakness of this measure is the social desirability effect according to which the student may wish to "fake good" on his answers to get a better score (Piers, 1984). High scores, therefore, can either indicate very good results or defensiveness and a desire to look good on the part of the student (Piers, 1984). However, the manual for the Piers-Harris scale provides extensive information about how to account for social desirability effects in scoring.

The teacher rating scale used in this study is a ten-item scale in Likert format with response choices on a five-point scale from weak = 1 to excellent = 5. Teachers complete the scale before and after the "I AM" group process (See Appendix C). Teachers rate students on ten items related to attendance, study/

work habits, homework completion, attentiveness, initiative, general behavior, overall academic achievement, leadership, respect for authority, and ability to work well with peers. This scale assesses how teachers perceive their students.

Statistical Analyses

A number of correlated t-tests were performed to examine the pre-post differences on the dependent measures of self-concept and teacher ratings for students in each of the three classrooms and for all three classrooms combined. The t-test for paired samples allowed the evaluator to determine if the "I AM" group process had a significant impact on students' self-concept and teacher ratings of student school-related behaviors and performance. The .01 and .05 levels of significance were used.

An analysis of covariance (ANCOVA) procedure was performed to see if there were any significant differences among the three class rooms. Pretest scores were used as covariates so that pot-test mean differences among the three classrooms could be examined after the pre-test differences were controlled statistically.

Results

The results of the paired sample t-tests revealed significant pre-post test changes for each classroom sample and for the three classrooms combined. (See tables 11.1–11.4)

Table 11.1. Classroom 1.

Dependent Variables	N	Mean Score for Pretest and Standard Deviation	Mean Score for Posttest and Standard Deviation	t	Sig
Behavior subscale of the Pier-Harris Self-Concept Scale	20	12.05 (3.19)	12.75 (3.04)	.751	.661
Intellectual and School Status Scale of the Piers-Harris Self-Concept Scale	20	13.10 (2.63)	13.65 (2.32)	.983	.026*
Behavior and Intellectual and School Status subscales combined	20	25.15 (5.29)	26.42 (4.44)	.988	.148
Teacher Rating Form	20	33.65 (8.86)	35.90 (8.64)	2.050	.000*

Note: * denotes significance.

Table 11.2.   Classroom 2.

Dependent Variables	N	Mean Score for Pretest and Standard Deviation	Mean Score for Posttest and Standard Deviation	t	Sig
Behavior subscale of the Pier-Harris Self-Concept Scale	16	12.19 (2.43)	13.00 (2.66)	1.119	.182
Intellectual and School Status Scale of the Piers-Harris Self-Concept Scale	16	12.81 (2.90)	12.54 (3.35)	.486	.001*
Behavior and Intellectual and School Status subscales combined	16	25.00 (4.59)	25.54 (4.72)	.636	.001*
Teacher Rating Form	16	35.82 (8.75)	39.50 (10.01)	1.946	.004*

Note: * denotes significance.

As indicated in table 11.1, the students in Classroom 1 showed significant improvement on the Intellectual and School Status subscale of the Piers-Harris Self-Concept Scale: mean pretest score = 13.10; mean posttest score = 13.65, t = .983 (df = 19), $p \leq .026$. The students in Classroom 1 also showed significant improvement in the teacher ratings that they received: mean pretest score = 33.65; mean posttest score = 35.90, t = 2.050 (DF = 19), $p \leq .000$

Table 11.3.   Classroom 3.

Dependent Variables	N	Mean Score for Pretest and Standard Deviation	Mean Score for Posttest and Standard Deviation	t	Sig
Behavior subscale of the Pier-Harris Self-Concept Scale	12	11.75 (1.96)	12.17 (2.21)	.635	.186
Intellectual and School Status Scale of the Piers-Harris Self-Concept Scale	12	12.92 (2.68)	12.92 (2.84)	.000	.001*
Behavior and Intellectual and School Status subscales combined	12	24.67 (3.47)	25.08 (3.82)	.546	.006*
Teacher Rating Form	12	36.92 (8.48)	38.17 (9.38)	1.196	.000*

Note: * denotes significance.

Table 11.4. All Three Classrooms Combined.

Dependent Variables	N	Mean Score for Pretest and Standard Deviation	Mean Score for Posttest and Standard Deviation	t	Sig
Behavior subscale of the Pier-Harris Self-Concept Scale	48	12.02 (2.63)	12.69 (2.69)	1.396	.122
Intellectual and School Status Scale of the Piers-Harris Self-Concept Scale	48	12.96 (2.68)	13.10 (2.81)	.433	.000*
Behavior and Intellectual and School Status subscales combined	48	24.98 (4.57)	25.78 (4.34)	1.300	.000*
Teacher Rating Form	48	35.19 (8.65)	37.67 (9.24)	3.035	.000*

Note: * denotes significance.

As indicated in table 11.2, the students in Classroom 2 showed significant improvement on the combined Behavior and Intellectual and School Status subscale of the Piers-Harris Self-Concept Scale: mean pretest score = 25.00; mean posttest score = 25.54, t = .636 (df = 15), $p \leq .001$. The students in Classroom 2 showed significant improvement on the teacher ratings that they received: mean pretest score = 35.82; mean posttest score = 39.50, t = 1.946 (DF = 15), $p \leq .004$. The students in Classroom 2 also showed a significant decrease in the mean score on the Intellectual and School Status subscale: mean pretest score = 12.81; mean posttest score = 12.54, t = .486 (df = 15), $p \leq .004$.

As indicated in table 11.3, the students in Classroom 3 showed significant improvement on the combined Behavior and Intellectual and School Status subscales of the Piers-Harris Self-Concept Scale: mean pretest score = 24.67; mean posttest score = 25.08, t = .546 (df = 11), $p \leq .006$. The students in Classroom 3 showed significant improvement on the teacher ratings that they received: mean pretest score = 36.92; mean posttest score = 38.17, t = 1.196 (DF = 11), $p \leq .000$. The students in Classroom 3 showed no change in mean scores on the Intellectual and School Status subscale: mean pretest score = 12.92; mean posttest score = 12.92, t = .000 (df = 11), $p \leq .001$.

As indicated in table 11.4, the students in all three classrooms showed significant improvement on the combined Behavior and Intellectual and School Status subscale of the Piers-Harris Self-Concept Scale: mean pretest score = 24.98; mean posttest score = 25.78, t = 1.300 (df = 47), $p \leq .000$. The students in all three classrooms showed significant improvement in the teacher ratings that they received: mean pretest score = 35.19; mean posttest score = 37.67, t = 3.035 (DF = 47), $p \leq .000$. The students in all three classrooms also showed significant improvement in mean scores on the Intellectual and School Status subscale: mean pretest score = 12.96; mean posttest score = 13.10, t = .433 (df = 47), $p \leq .000$. The ANCOVA revealed no significant classroom effects. There were no significant differences in scores among the three classrooms.

Discussion

During class discussions, students expressed positive feelings about reciting affirmations and usually recited them with enthusiasm. Observing students during the group process, it appeared that the group was having some positive impact on the students' feelings and outlook. This could be seen in the enthusiasm and happiness that many students expressed at the start of each "I AM" group process and by the comments students made during and at the end of the group process. Students generally expressed the view that while the classroom experience did not improve 100% after each group process, there was an improvement in their overall feeling of academic self-concept and in their attitudes toward learning. In a few cases, some students seemed to remain unaffected by the experience. Generally, students were more aware of the positive impact of saying affirmations and recognizing their strengths.

In general, it seemed that the group process either had a positive impact or no significant impact. It appeared that students with extremely low self-concepts did not change significantly. The same seemed to hold true for students with extremely high self-concepts. They showed no significant decline. The one exception was for Classroom 2, which had a significant decrease in the mean score for the Intellectual and School Status subscale of the Piers-Harris Self-Concept Scale. Because there may have been factors beyond the scope of this study affecting both the improvement and decrease in mean scores for all students on the posttests, it is not clear what may have accounted for the decrease in the mean score for the Intellectual and School Status subscale for students Classroom 2. It is quite possible that there were classroom events and experiences not controlled for in this evaluation study that may have been responsible. It is also quite possible that the "I AM" group process was not effective enough to positively impact this area of self-concept for the students in Classroom 2.

It is notable that the scores for the Piers-Harris Behavior Scale did not significantly change over time for all three classrooms, as indicated by the paired samples t-test scores. However, the scores did change significantly on the Intellectual and School Status scale. This makes sense given that the "I AM" group had a strong focus on academic skills and positive self-concept in school and achievement oriented activities. In addition, teacher rating scors for all three groups also exhibited a significant change over time.

The results of the ANCOVA revealed no significant differences among the posttest scores for all three classrooms once the pretest differences were taken into account. Thus, it is assumed that the "I AM" group process had similar effects across all three groups. Despite the fact that each classroom had a different teacher, classroom culture, and classroom setting, it seems that the "I AM" group process positively affected students in all three classes in some way. Classroom differences, in fact, can be one of the factors that explained why each class had differing significant changes in posttest scores for the Intellectual and School Status Scale. One class showed improvement, one class had a decrease in scores, and the last class showed no overall improvement on average.

The only factor that could confound the validity of the teacher rating scores would be if the teachers, knowing that this group was supposed to have a positive effect, made all the scores higher in the post assessment so that there would be a significant difference between pre and post test scores. However, if the group process was not having any positive effect, it seems safe to assume that the teachers would not be as willing to make the rating scores deliberately higher. Most students seemed to have answered questions honestly because most were willing to give socially undesirable answers. That can be credited to the complete confidentially of the test scores having been stressed.

Future studies could include a qualitative analysis as well as a quantitative analysis in order to get further information about pre and post effects of similar psycho-educational group interventions. For example, focus groups after the group process has ended can provide information about how students and teachers feel about the class and how they feel the class affected them. While there were discussions at the end of each group process about these topics, the discussions were informal and not in the form of structured focus groups. Children and teachers gave positive feedback which was not captured in the data analysis.

Some feedback suggested that perhaps this process would be more effective as a semester- long or even year-long motivational process that would be better incorporated into the class curriculum. However, this study and past studies have shown that short-term group processes can have a significant effect if implemented properly (Page & Chandler, 1994). Page and Chandler (1994) had significant results after conducting two different self-concept enhancing groups that each ran for 2 hours per week for 10 weeks. It is a question of how long the group process is, how well it is implemented, and what outside factors could be affecting the student sample.

Another weakness of this evaluation study was that it was not possible to obtain a control group because the principal required that this group process be performed equally with all the fourth-grade classrooms. Therefore, it was not possible to compare treatment groups to non-treatment groups to see if there might be any significant differences in group process outcomes.

Given the positive, significant results gained from this evaluation study, it is suggested that future evaluation research examine the effects of this motivational group with students in other grades. The curriculum can be modified to address the needs of different grade levels without sacrificing the main purpose and goals of the group process: to increase positive self-concept.

As was experienced in this study, it may be difficult to obtain a control group within the same school because teachers and principals may want all of their classrooms to have the same treatment and assessment. It may be possible and desirable to obtain a control group in another school with a similar population. However, such a strategy may face challenges given that it may be difficult to find a similar group or a school that would allow a researcher to examine a group without an intervention.

Future researchers may also want to develop an all-year curriculum and compare the results to that of the established 8 week group process. Students who often experience fragmented or short-lived relationships in life can benefit from yearlong support. Also, children always seem sad when a significant, positive adult in their life leaves too quickly for their liking.

It is also suggested that teachers may wish to incorporate the "I AM" strategies into their classroom. Teachers can choose to use the "I AM" group process for either the entire class or for a small, select group of students and are encouraged to assess the progress of students who participate in the "I AM" group process.

Chapter Twelve

Theoretical Perspectives and Ethical and Legal Considerations

THEORETICAL PERSPECTIVES

Group leaders and facilitators are sometimes guided by their theoretical orientations when facilitating groups. Many of the main theoretical perspectives that are applied to individual counseling also apply to group counseling as well. Some of the main perspectives may be classified as *behaviorist, humanistic, psychoanalytic or cognitive*. These perspectives are briefly explained below.

Behavioral

These approaches emphasize the relationship between a stimulus and a response and consider the important role that experience plays in learning. The basic therapeutic approach is to help the client to identify and describe problem behaviors, identify antecedent conditions that trigger or activate the problem behaviors, and to examine and address the consequences to ultimately change the problem behaviors. The operational model in the behavioral approach is presented as Antecedent Behavior Consequence (A-B-C). The therapeutic position is that one needs to change the antecedents and consequences to change behavior. This approach also places emphasis on instrumental or operant learning, associated with B. F. Skinner, which is the notion that behaviors are learned through reinforcement in the form of rewards for desirable or expected behavior and that undesirable behavior is unlearned through extinction (the removal of reinforcement) or through punishing the undesired behavior.

The classical learning paradigm, associated with Ivan Pavlov, is also applied in behavioral approaches. This is the notion that behaviors are sometimes learned through principles of conditioning based on the association of stimuli or activating events and generalization of behavior from one of the associated events to the other. In the group process the emphasis then would be on observable, describable, concrete behavior change, applying learning principles to bring about the needed change.

Cognitive-Behavioral and Rational Emotive

These approaches are premised on the notion that the stimulus response paradigm of the behavioral approaches leaves out an essential ingredient that influences human behavior. According to Cognitive Behavioral Therapy (CBT) the missing ingredient is cognition in the form of thoughts and beliefs about the antecedents or activating events and about the consequences that may follow the behavior. Therefore, rather than Antecedent Behavior and Consequence as in the Behavioral approach, there is *A*ntecedent *C*ognition *B*ehavior *C*onsequence (ACBC). The notion is that faulty cognitions result is maladaptive behaviors that can have undesirable consequences. In order to change maladaptive behaviors, individuals need to change their cognitions. In addition to cognition, Rational-Emotive Therapy (RET) developed by Albert Ellis includes and emphasizes the importance of the relationship between thinking, emotions and behavior. This may be represented as *A*ntecedent *C*ognition *E*motion *B*ehavior *C*onsequence (ACEBC).

In situations, the manner in which an event is perceived and processed influences how the individual feels about the event which, in turn, affects how the individual reacts to the event. The therapist's role in these approaches is to help the individual analyze their cognitions: beliefs, thoughts and perceptions, about an event or experience, change these cognitions that may be irrational and counterproductive. In the context of groups, the goal is to help group members explore their thinking about experiences and events through group interaction, sharing and giving and receiving feedback. The group leader may be more directive and more confrontational than in some other groups.

Humanistic

Humanistic approaches focus attention on the meaning of one's existence and on the notion that the individual has the potential to become a better person and to become more fulfilled. Three of the most widely used approaches are the Adlerian, Person-Centered or Rogerian and the Gestalt.

Adlerian

This approach was developed by Alfred Adler and is premised on the belief that human beings are continually evolving and seeking to become fulfilled persons. The basic premise is that human beings are always "becoming," continually moving toward the future, and concerned with subjective goals more than objective realities. As such, they are oriented toward the future and not the past. The individual focuses on his or her subjective goals. Individuals are continually striving towards what Adler called superiority. This can lead to unrealistic or unattainable goals, behaviors that are self-defeating and feelings of discouragement may develop. The role of the therapist is to help the client identify mistaken goals, and to help the client do away with self-centeredness, egotism, and isolation, and to develop positive, meaningful interpersonal relationships. In the context of the group, generally, the group sessions involve listening, questioning and understanding the goals of group members. Group members seek to know one another as well as possible and to provide constructive feedback to one another in helping to examine and reformulate personal goals.

Person-Centered (Rogerian)

This approach was developed by Carl Rogers who believed that everyone is in the process of becoming and has the potential to become self-actualized or self-fulfilled by reaching his or her potential. Rogers believed that the individuals' early life experiences may have alienated the individual from his or her true self-potential. The key element in the therapeutic process is the client-therapist relationship. The therapist creates conditions that support the client's growth through understanding, empathy, genuineness, and unconditional positive regard. The goal is to help the client move toward self-actualization. In the context of group counseling and therapy, the group leader helps to create a climate in which group members receive empathy, understanding and unconditional positive regard with encouragement to recognize their self-worth and to move toward self-actualizing their potential.

Gestalt Therapy

This approach was developed by Fritz Perls. The word "gestalt," is a German word that means "whole." The premise is that in present-day society, people become fragmented, disconnected from others, feel pulled in too many directions and begin to feel that they are not grounded. The goal is to help individuals achieve a sense of wholeness; an integration of the various parts of the self. The focus is on the here and now. Individuals are held responsible for their own well-being through being always fully aware of all aspects of themselves and being fully cognizant of their interactions with others and with the environment. Individuals are encouraged to change how they express their behavior and to change their language' for example from "I cannot" to "I would not" and from "I should do this" to "I have decided to do this." The rephrasing shows an acceptance of responsibility. In the context of groups, the goal is to help the group members to become more fully aware of who they are, of their needs and their feelings. Group members are encouraged to pay attention to all aspects of themselves including their breathing, body posture and body movements. The gestalt group tends to be very experiential involving an array of physical and sensory activities and enactments, role plays and "experiments" Unresolved issues and conflicts are addressed and worked through in the group session as though they are happening in the present.

Psychoanalytic

This approach is identified mainly with Sigmund Freud and focuses on exploring the unconscious mind to identify, analyze and address the root causes of behavior and feelings. As indicated in chapter four during the discussion of the JOHARI window, there is the unconscious quadrant that is the intersection between what "I do not know about myself" and what "others do not know about me" that is the repository of hidden and unknown motivations and drives that fuel unexplained behavior. The goal of therapy is to help the client access unconscious motives and drives and to confront maladaptive defense mechanisms that the ego uses to protect itself. The therapist may use such psychodynamic techniques as dream analysis, free-association, and transference, to help the individual gain a better understanding of their own minds. In the context of the group, group members are encouraged to explore past experiences and repressed memories and feelings to achieve catharsis and healing.

ETHICAL AND LEGAL CONSIDERATIONS

Ethical and legal issues in group work, as in individual counseling and therapy must be carefully considered and taken seriously by group leaders and facilitators. Sometimes ethical and legal issues intersect and the violation of one sometimes may mean the violation of the other. Below is a discussion of some key ethical and legal considerations.

Confidentiality

This is a very basic and essential ethical and legal consideration. The information that group members share about their backgrounds, experiences and issues and the interactions among group members are to be treated strictly confidential to be disclosed only if sharing such information is necessary to prevent and avert imminent danger to a group member or group members from self or others, or if such information is subpoenaed by a court of law. In addition to being an ethical and legal issue, the knowledge by group members that confidentiality is a guiding principle and norm for the group helps to create a climate of trust and safety among members of the group. The legality of confidentiality rests in the fact that disclosure of privileged information is a violation of an explicit or implicit contract to protect the privacy rights of group members.

Competence

The competence of the group leader and facilitator is both an ethical and a legal consideration. Just as the counselors and therapists who work with individuals are expected to practice only in their areas of competence and to maintain current credentials and updated skills, so too, group practitioners must ensure that they are properly qualified and prepared to lead and facilitate the groups that they do. The ethics of this issue has to do with the professional responsibility that the group leader has to the group members. The legality of this issue of competence has to do with the potential for civil liability or even criminal liability of malpractice in the event that group members are in any way endangered physically, psychologically or emotionally during the group process.

Dual Relationships

The group leader, just like the therapist in an individual counseling relationship with a single client, is in a power relationship with the members of the group in that the group leader is respected, trusted and to some extent depended on emotionally, by members of the group. Any other relationship that compromises the integrity of the therapeutic relationship in the group is a violation of the group's trust and places the group members involved in the non-therapeutic relationship in a disadvantaged position. The ethics of this issue has to do with the potential for an abuse of power (legitimate power) by the group leader. The legality has to do with the potential for violation of group members' civil rights.

Consent

It is the responsibility of the group leader to obtain appropriate written consent from group members before they participate in a therapeutic group process. This is an ethical consideration that protects both the group leader and the group members from the appearance of or potential charge of coercion with regard to participation in the group process. When children and adolescents who are minors are involved in a group process, it is necessary to obtain written consent from the parents or legal guardians of the minors.

Social, Cultural and Physical Diversity

Every group leader has a responsibility to be aware of, be sensitive to and to respond appropriately to the diverse and unique needs of group members from various social and cultural subgroups who may be participating in the group process. The group's diversity may be based on race, ethnicity, culture, religion, sexual preference or physical disability. The use of stereotypical references, prejudicial comments or other offensive language or actions may not only interfere with the integrity of the group process but also violate the dignity, pride and rights of the offended group members. Making appropriate accommodations for those with physical challenges is also an ethical and legal responsibility of the group leader.

Index

CPSIA information can be obtained at www.ICGtesting.com
Printed in the USA
BVOW070836141211

278292BV00002B/5/P

Printed in Great Britain
by Amazon.co.uk, Ltd.,
Marston Gate.